MICHAEL
JORDAN

———— ❦ ————

MICHAEL JORDAN

Sean Dolan

Senior Consulting Editor
Nathan Irvin Huggins
Director
W. E. B. Dubois Institute for Afro-American Research
Harvard University

CHELSEA HOUSE PUBLISHERS
New York   Philadelphia

Chelsea House Publishers
Editorial Director Richard Rennert
Executive Managing Editor Karyn Gullen Browne
Executive Editor Sean Dolan
Copy Chief Robin James
Picture Editor Adrian G. Allen
Art Director Robert Mitchell
Manufacturing Director Gerald Levine
Systems Manager Lindsey Ottman
Production Coordinator Marie Claire Cebrián-Ume

Black Americans of Achievement
Senior Editor Sean Dolan

Staff for MICHAEL JORDAN
Editorial Assistant Joy Sanchez
Designer John Infantino
Picture Researcher Patricia Burns
Cover Illustrator Daniel O'Leary

Copyright © 1994 by Chelsea House Publishers, a division of Main
Line Book Co. All rights reserved. Printed and bound in the United
States of America.

3 5 7 9 8 6 4

Library of Congress Cataloging-in-Publication Data
Dolan, Sean.
    Michael Jordan, basketball great/Sean Dolan
        p. cm.—(Black Americans of achievement)
    Includes bibliographical references (p.) and index.
ISBN   0-7910-2150-5
        0-7910-2151-3 (pbk.)
    1. Jordan, Michael, 1963—Juvenile literature. 2. Basketball
players—United States—Biography—Juvenile literature. I. Title.
II. Series.
GV884.J63D65 1993   93-16714
796.323'092—dc20   CIP
[B]   AC

*Frontispiece: Michael Jordan pursues
a loose ball. Not even his dangling
tongue detracts from Jordan's on-court
gracefulness.*

CONTENTS

BLACK AMERICANS OF ACHIEVEMENT

HENRY AARON
baseball great

KAREEM ABDUL-JABBAR
basketball great

RALPH ABERNATHY
civil rights leader

ALVIN AILEY
choreographer

MUHAMMAD ALI
heavyweight champion

RICHARD ALLEN
*religious leader and
social activist*

MAYA ANGELOU
author

LOUIS ARMSTRONG
musician

ARTHUR ASHE
tennis great

JOSEPHINE BAKER
entertainer

JAMES BALDWIN
author

BENJAMIN BANNEKER
scientist and mathematician

AMIRI BARAKA
poet and playwright

COUNT BASIE
bandleader and composer

ROMARE BEARDEN
artist

JAMES BECKWOURTH
frontiersman

MARY MCLEOD BETHUNE
educator

JULIAN BOND
civil rights leader and politician

GWENDOLYN BROOKS
poet

JIM BROWN
football great

RALPH BUNCHE
diplomat

STOKELY CARMICHAEL
civil rights leader

GEORGE WASHINGTON
CARVER
botanist

RAY CHARLES
musician

CHARLES CHESNUTT
author

JOHN COLTRANE
musician

BILL COSBY
entertainer

PAUL CUFFE
merchant and abolitionist

COUNTEE CULLEN
poet

BENJAMIN DAVIS, SR., AND
BENJAMIN DAVIS, JR.
military leaders

SAMMY DAVIS, JR.
entertainer

FATHER DIVINE
religious leader

FREDERICK DOUGLASS
abolitionist editor

CHARLES DREW
physician

W. E. B. DU BOIS
scholar and activist

PAUL LAURENCE DUNBAR
poet

KATHERINE DUNHAM
dancer and choreographer

DUKE ELLINGTON
bandleader and composer

RALPH ELLISON
author

JULIUS ERVING
basketball great

JAMES FARMER
civil rights leader

ELLA FITZGERALD
singer

MARCUS GARVEY
black nationalist leader

JOSH GIBSON
baseball great

DIZZY GILLESPIE
musician

WHOOPI GOLDBERG
entertainer

ALEX HALEY
author

PRINCE HALL
social reformer

MATTHEW HENSON
explorer

CHESTER HIMES
author

BILLIE HOLIDAY
singer

LENA HORNE
entertainer

LANGSTON HUGHES
poet

ZORA NEALE HURSTON
author

JESSE JACKSON
civil rights leader and politician

MICHAEL JACKSON
entertainer

JACK JOHNSON
heavyweight champion

JAMES WELDON JOHNSON
author

MAGIC JOHNSON
basketball great

SCOTT JOPLIN
composer

BARBARA JORDAN
politician

MICHAEL JORDAN
basketball great

CORETTA SCOTT KING
civil rights leader

MARTIN LUTHER KING, JR.
civil rights leader

LEWIS LATIMER
scientist

SPIKE LEE
filmmaker

CARL LEWIS
champion athlete

JOE LOUIS
heavyweight champion

RONALD MCNAIR
astronaut

MALCOLM X
militant black leader

THURGOOD MARSHALL
Supreme Court justice

TONI MORRISON
author

ELIJAH MUHAMMAD
religious leader

EDDIE MURPHY
entertainer

JESSE OWENS
champion athlete

SATCHEL PAIGE
baseball great

CHARLIE PARKER
musician

GORDON PARKS
photographer

ROSA PARKS
civil rights leader

SIDNEY POITIER
actor

ADAM CLAYTON
POWELL, JR.
political leader

COLIN POWELL
military leader

LEONTYNE PRICE
opera singer

A. PHILIP RANDOLPH
labor leader

PAUL ROBESON
singer and actor

JACKIE ROBINSON
baseball great

DIANA ROSS
entertainer

BILL RUSSELL
basketball great

JOHN RUSSWURM
publisher

SOJOURNER TRUTH
antislavery activist

HARRIET TUBMAN
antislavery activist

NAT TURNER
slave revolt leader

DENMARK VESEY
slave revolt leader

ALICE WALKER
author

MADAM C. J. WALKER
entrepreneur

BOOKER T. WASHINGTON
educator and racial spokesman

IDA WELLS-BARNETT
civil rights leader

WALTER WHITE
civil rights leader

OPRAH WINFREY
entertainer

STEVIE WONDER
musician

RICHARD WRIGHT
author

ON
ACHIEVEMENT

Coretta Scott King

BEFORE YOU BEGIN this book, I hope you will ask yourself what the word *excellence* means to you. I think that it's a question we should all ask, and keep asking as we grow older and change. Because the truest answer to it should never change. When you think of excellence, perhaps you think of success at work; or of becoming wealthy; or meeting the right person, getting married, and having a good family life.

Those important goals are worth striving for, but there is a better way to look at excellence. As Martin Luther King, Jr., said in one of his last sermons, "I want you to be first in love. I want you to be first in moral excellence. I want you to be first in generosity. If you want to be important, wonderful. If you want to be great, wonderful. But recognize that he who is greatest among you shall be your servant."

My husband, Martin Luther King, Jr., knew that the true meaning of achievement is service. When I met him in 1952 he was already ordained as a Baptist preacher and was working toward a doctoral degree at Boston University. I was studying at the New England Conservatory and dreamed of accomplishments in music. We married a year later, and after I graduated the following year we moved to Montgomery, Alabama. We didn't know it then, but our notions of achievement were about to undergo a dramatic change.

You may have read or heard about what happened next. What began with the boycott of a local bus line grew into a national movement, and by the time he was assassinated in 1968 my husband had fashioned a black movement powerful enough to shatter forever the practice of racial segregation. What you may not have read about is where he got his method for resisting injustice without compromising his religious beliefs.

He adopted the strategy of nonviolence from a man of a different race, who lived in a different country, and even practiced a different religion. The man was Mahatma Gandhi, the great leader of India, who devoted his life to serving humanity in the spirit of love and nonviolence. It was in these principles that Martin discovered his method for social reform. More than anything else, those two principles were the key to his achievements.

This book is about black Americans who served society through the excellence of their achievements. It forms a part of the rich history of black men and women in America—a history of stunning accomplishments in every field of human endeavor, from literature and art to science, industry, education, diplomacy, athletics, jurisprudence, even polar exploration.

Not all of the people in this history had the same ideals, but I think you will find something that all of them had in common. Like Martin Luther King, Jr., they all decided to become "drum majors" and serve humanity. In that principle—whether it was expressed in books, inventions, or song—they found something outside themselves to use as a goal and a guide. Something that showed them a way to serve others, instead of only living for themselves.

Reading the stories of these courageous men and women not only helps us discover the principles that we will use to guide our own lives but also teaches us about our black heritage and about America itself. It is crucial for us to know the heroes and heroines of our history and to realize that the price we paid in our struggle for equality in America was dear. But we must also understand that we have gotten as far as we have partly because America's democratic system and ideals made it possible.

We are still struggling with racism and prejudice. But the great men and women in this series are a tribute to the spirit of our democratic ideals and the system in which they have flourished. And that makes their stories special and worth knowing. ◊

1

THE JORDAN RULES

❧

CAN A PLAYER be too good? Very few athletes ever have to grapple with such a question. Nobody ever suggested that Carl Lewis ought not to run so fast (except those who trailed behind him as he broke the finishing tape, of course), and Babe Ruth was rarely asked to bunt. It was seldom hinted to O. J. Simpson that perhaps his team might be better off if he let someone else carry the ball for a change, and Wayne Gretzky's record-breaking performances immediately earned him the nickname of "the Great One." But as regarded Michael Jordan, the six-foot-six-inch All-League guard for the National Basketball Association's Chicago Bulls, the question was a most relevant one in May 1990 as his team prepared for the Eastern Conference Finals playoff series with their archrival, the Detroit Pistons, the league's defending champion.

Michael Jordan dunks for two points in a playoff game with the Detroit Pistons in May 1988. Though nondescript by Jordan's spectacular standards, this basket was noteworthy for one reason: Detroit rarely left Jordan so unattended.

The question was both tribute to Jordan's unparalleled abilities as a basketball player and commentary on the nature of the game he played. That spring, he had completed his sixth regular season in the National Basketball Association (NBA) and had won his fourth-straight scoring championship. His career scoring average was above 30 points per game—20 points per game is the traditional benchmark of scoring excellence in the NBA—and his scoring average in the playoffs, the time when the true measure of a professional basketball player's merit is gauged, soared even higher, to nearly 35 points per game. No player as small—six-feet-six is considered only average size for an NBA player—had ever scored so prolifically, and only one, the graceful behemoth Wilt Chamberlain, had ever matched Jordan's season scoring marks. (In 1993, Jordan would match Chamberlain's record of leading the NBA in scoring for seven straight years, and his points-per-game average for the regular season, the playoffs, and the All-Star Game is the highest in NBA history.)

No one had ever scored so much, and no one had ever scored so spectacularly. In a league ruled by the world's greatest athletes—all of them possessing an improbable combination of size, speed, quickness, jumping ability, strength, and stamina, and the best of them also owning qualities of intelligence and intuition that set them apart from their merely physically gifted counterparts—Jordan was unique in every way.

At first glance he appeared slight, even spindly, in comparison with the league's more sculpted physiques, but when he was in motion long, ropy muscles stood out in relief against every inch of his lithe body, and those in his thin legs propelled him to stratospheric heights. He was the highest flying of the league's many celebrated leapers, earner of the nickname Air for the element where he seemed to spend most of his on-court time, and the most graceful—despite his childlike habit of leaving his tongue dangling from his open mouth—of its balletic improvisers. His dunks were legend; observers swore they saw him change direction in mid-flight, and his serpentine drives dominated the league's highlight reels. Traumatized defenders were grateful when he settled for a jump shot, but he was, of course, an outstanding outside shooter who regularly drained more than half of his shots. (Fifty percent is considered an exceptional shooting percentage, especially for a guard.) Though it was said—wishfully, perhaps—that because of his slight frame he could be slowed by bullying defensive tactics, he had (discounting his second year in the league, in which a broken foot kept him on the sidelines for much of the season) missed only one game in his entire career,

Using the rim to shield him from his defender, Jordan completes a reverse lay-up with his left hand. Perhaps no player in the history of the National Basketball Association (NBA) has had as many different—and thrilling—ways to score.

a record of durability unmatched by any of the game's reigning superstars. His best performances seemed often to come when he was supposedly hampered by a sprained ankle or the flu or any of the myriad nagging injuries and illnesses to which overworked NBA players are prone. "There are a lot of guys in the league who perform spectacular feats," said long-time NBA coach Bill Fitch. "They do it once. Michael does a steady diet of it. Every game, every practice." After seeing Jordan play just a few times, Frank Layden, then coach of the Utah Jazz, said, "The way he goes flying through the air, gets knocked down . . . I said 'Come April and this guy is going to be dead. He won't have anything left in the playoffs.' You know what? He's better in the playoffs."

But because basketball is the truest team sport played professionally in the United States, the achievements of its greatest scorers are often evaluated with a certain skepticism. Scoring is the most glamorous part of basketball; it is the most easily understood facet of the game, and the most easily quantified, and at virtually every level at which basketball is played the high scorers are the most celebrated and most highly rewarded players. Scoring average is the easiest way to measure a player's value and accomplishments, but it is seldom the truest, simply because of the nature of the game itself: though the object of the game is to score points, more often than not it is in a team's interest for a player to decide not to try to do so. In no other sport is an individual required to make so many decisions relevant to his team's immediate effort to score; in no other sport is individual freedom as dominant a variable; no other sport requires such a sublimation of individual initiative to a common goal.

The quandary of any basketball team is simple: the team needs to score. All five players on the court for a team at any single time would like to do so, but only one at a time can. Some of the players must therefore sacrifice their individual desires for the good of the team—to derive their satisfaction from winning rather than from scoring. Ideally, all five players on the floor for a team at any given time are less concerned with *who* scores than with how their team is faring. On the professional level, where compensation, celebrity, status, playing time, and livelihood are often directly related to a player's scoring average, and where questions of human nature, jealousy, and ego are thus more greatly involved, the task of creating a winning team becomes even more difficult. "Basketball," the longtime NBA guard and coach John Lucas is fond of saying, "is a very simple game played by very complicated people."

For Jordan, the dilemmas thus posed were unique, as one might expect in regard to such a singular talent. In the NBA, stardom and riches are the rewards for high scorers, but the ultimate acclaim is reserved for winners—those whose teams win a championship. The two goals are often not compatible; many NBA stars, consciously or not, have opted for gaudy statistics, hefty paychecks, and the fans' acclaim at the expense of their team's success. (Rightly or wrongly, Chamberlain, for one, was often accused of being more interested in personal statistical accomplishments than in his team's success.)

By 1990, Jordan's individual basketball achievements were unmatched, he was the league's most popular player and biggest box-office draw, and he earned more from commercial endorsements than any athlete in American history. Yet he was not accorded quite the same level of respect as the league's true reigning royalty—Larry Bird of the Boston Celtics and Earvin "Magic" Johnson of the Los Angeles Lakers, for Bird's Celtics had won three championships in the 1980s, and Magic's five championship rings and eight trips to the finals during that same decade had become the standard by which this generation of the NBA measured excellence.

Jordan's positive effect on his team's fortunes was undeniable—in his first year, he had led a selfish, ragtag collection of ball hogs, journeymen, substance abusers, and sex offenders to the playoffs; Chicago has never since failed to make the playoffs, and by 1990 the Bulls were considered one of the league's elite squads—yet there were many who believed that with him Chicago would never make the transformation to true championship caliber. Jordan's critics—and there were many—were always quick to point out that no player had ever led the league in scoring and played on a championship team in the same season.

Jordan guards the winningest player of his generation, Earvin "Magic" Johnson, in the low post. By 1990, injuries had begun to diminish Larry Bird's game, leaving Johnson, whose Los Angeles Lakers had won five NBA championships, as Jordan's only true rival for the title of best basketball player in the world. Though not Jordan's equal as a scorer or defender, Johnson was at that time generally rated the superior player by virtue of his passing skills and leadership qualities.

For Jordan, the criticism rankled, for though immensely proud of his scoring ability and not without a considerable ego—"I always wanted my teams to do well, but I always wanted to be the main cause," he said once early in his professional career—he was neither selfish nor a one-dimensional gunner. In several seasons, he had led the Bulls in rebounds and assists as well as in scoring, and he was a superb defensive player, customarily among the league's leaders in steals and often tops among guards in blocked shots. In the 1987–88 season, he had become the first player to win the NBA's Most Valuable Player (MVP) Award and Defensive Player of the Year Award in the same season. (He remains the only player to have accomplished that particular feat; in fact, no one has ever garnered those two accolades over the course of their career, let alone in a single season.) Like his shotmaking, his passing often approached the level of artistry; he possessed that rare combination of intuition, anticipation, and vision that allowed him to see order in the shifting, kaleidoscopic welter of huge bodies jostling for position on the cramped confines of the hardwood and immediately deliver the ball to an open teammate.

Yet the criticism persisted: Michael shot too much and scored too much for the Bulls ever to win a championship, and he was unwilling to reign in that aspect of his game in order to allow Chicago to develop a more balanced scoring attack. Through their passing and unselfish play, the argument went, Bird and Johnson made their teammates better, but Jordan's style rewarded only himself; though he passed well, he did not pass enough. That Jordan had never played with teammates the caliber of those who had taken the court with the great Celtic and Laker stalwarts was often overlooked. Besides Bird and Johnson, every other member of the starting fives of the great Boston and Los Angeles teams of the mid-1980s was an All-Star at some time in his career, and five of those eight will in all likelihood be voted into basketball's Hall of Fame one day. To that point in his professional career, Jordan had not yet played with a teammate of All-Star caliber.

So from Jordan's point of view, he scored less out of desire than out of need—because that was what was required from him in order for his team to win. He was shouldering a tremendous burden—the belief that unless he scored a minimum of 30 points a game, his team had little chance of victory—yet it seemed he was criticized for the very magnitude of his talent. As the league's quintessential franchise player, he bore the greatest share of responsibility for his team's success, yet he was constantly being asked to put constraints on his game, to defer, to a larger extent than he deemed prudent, to demonstrably less talented and willing teammates. For lesser players, the decision between sacrifice and scoring was perhaps more easily made, for none could realistically take the court, as did Jordan every night, with the self-assurance that he was the best player on it.

Yet, as several of Jordan's coaches pointed out, his very greatness seemed ultimately, for his team, to be self-defeating. At times, Jordan did so much—scoring, rebounding, blocking shots, bringing the ball up court—that his teammates were reduced to the role of spectators. So accustomed did they become to relying on him to bail them out of every tight spot, and so frightened were some of them by the prospect of living up to his impossibly high standards, that in tight contests—and especially in the crucible of the playoffs—their play became tentative and fearful. (Like many talented individuals, Jordan found it very difficult to understand why others could not do what he could, and he could be quite cutting in expressing his displeasure.) It had become a vicious circle: the more Michael did, the less confident his teammates became about their own ability to contribute, and their play grew the poorer for it; the less confident his teammates appeared, and the poorer their play, the more Michael felt he had to do himself.

His greatness even presented problems in practice. Jordan was so good that one of his coaches had adopted the tactic of making him change teams in the middle of intrasquad games. Invariably, Jordan's team would jump out to a huge lead, at which point he would be ordered to transfer to the losing side, which then usually overtook the other. When he went all out defensively—and Jordan, who is, by all accounts, fanatically competitive, found it difficult to let up even in practice—he was capable of so disrupting offensive drills that they became essentially worthless. Chicago usually reserved a place on its roster for a player whose primary purpose was to be Jordan's practice fodder—that is, one whose ego was strong enough to withstand the daily humiliation of going one-on-one with the game's greatest player and who would continue to practice hard, providing Jordan with at least a modicum of competition. Those players usually ended the season with their confidence totally shattered and were seldom of much use in the league again.

"During the first drills and everything, that's when I figured out he was so competitive," said Chicago forward Cliff Levingston, who was new to the team in 1990. "I said to Craig [Hodges, another teammate], 'Is he always like this?' He said, 'Man, he hates to lose. Hates to lose. And you can't give him anything. Don't let him have his way with you or he will look down on you.'" After watching Jordan dismantle a free-agent aspirant to the Bulls, Craig Neal, in a preseason defensive drill, Chicago assistant coach John Bach observed that "Craig saw the fury that is Michael" and spoke of the "swelling pride that is in the man."

If Jordan was often frustrated with his teammates' shortcomings, his fellow Bulls were equally disconcerted by the knowledge that no matter how hard they tried, they could never match his abilities or satisfy his expectations. "It's hard playing on a team with Michael Jordan," said onetime Bulls center Dave Corzine, "because you're always the reason the team lost." Jordan's "supporting cast," as he sometimes uncharitably referred to his teammates, alternately chafed at the lack of opportunity to do more on the court or relaxed into a "let Michael do it" attitude. Even Jordan's coaches confessed to an unhealthy reliance on his preternatural abilities. In the closing moments of tight games, Bach once confessed, the Bulls often turned to what he laughingly termed the "archangel offense"—"that's where we give Jordan the ball and say 'Michael, save us'"—rather than to better-conceived offensive schemes.

Jordan's heroics were enough to carry his team through the regular season and to a certain point in the playoffs, but there was one obstacle that even Superman had not yet been able to surmount—the Detroit Pistons. Detroit had eliminated Chicago from the playoffs in the spring of 1988 and the spring of 1989. In May 1990 the two teams were meeting for the second straight year in the Eastern Conference finals, with the winner of the best-of-seven series to go on to contest for the NBA championship with the Western Conference representative. There was little reason to believe that the Bulls would fare any better against the Pistons this time out.

Chicago was coming off its most successful regular season of the Jordan era. Their 55 wins in 82 games gave the Bulls the league's second-best record, but the best record—59 wins—belonged to the defending-champion Pistons, who thus finished four games ahead of the Bulls in their own division, and Detroit had handily defeated Chicago in four of five

No team made Jordan work harder for his points than the Detroit Pistons. Though the Bulls' star has here succeeded in splitting a double team by Pistons guards Isiah Thomas (at right) and Joe Dumars (behind Jordan), Detroit's relentless physical assault kept him consistently off balance.

regular-season contests. There was, moreover, no reason to expect that the tactics Detroit had used with such great success against Chicago in the past would not continue to be effective.

The Pistons were the league's outlaws. In a league that prided itself on the speed, grace, aerial acrobatics, and offensive skills of its athletes, the Pistons were brawny, slow, earthbound, and defensive minded. They were the best defensive team the league had ever seen, but they shut down opponents with a bruising, excessively physical—many said dirty—style that stretched the letter and spirit of the rule book to its breaking point. The Pistons positively reveled in their self-styled image as the Bad Boys of the NBA; they clutched and grabbed, they held, they elbowed, they undercut, and when they fouled they fouled hard, hoping thereby to intimidate opponents or at least sap their determination. Their aim was to slow the pace of each game to a virtual crawl, to turn each game into the professional-basketball equivalent of a street brawl—a style that was especially frustrating to Jordan and the Bulls, who flourished when the premium was on quickness and finesse. If Detroit's style was less than aesthetically pleasing, it was also most effective.

And under their mastermind, head coach Chuck Daly, the Pistons had developed a special set of tactics devised specifically for games against Chicago—the so-called Jordan Rules. Created after Jordan scorched the Pistons for 59 points in a Chicago victory on

The Jordan Rules enacted: Pistons Dennis Rodman (left) and Tree Rollins (center, wearing number 30) aid Dumars (number 4) with Jordan. Such tactics left several of Jordan's teammates unguarded, of course, but Detroit was willing to take such a risk in order to make Jordan give up the basketball or take a bad shot.

Easter Sunday in 1988, the rules were born of what would seem to have been the exceedingly obvious fact that, as Daly put it, in Jordan "you are talking about the ultimate scorer in basketball. You have to have some kind of defensive plan. One person can't do it. You've got to use three or four."

As diagrammed by Daly and his assistants, the Jordan Rules broke down into 13 separate defensive sets, but their essence was simple. All five defensive players had to be aware of where Jordan was at all times; he was to be double-teamed each time he touched the ball; and he was to be funnelled toward the middle of the floor when he made his move toward the basket.

On the surface, this last tactic seemed to be counterproductive, for Jordan preferred to work the middle of the floor, where he had more room to operate and thus more freedom to improvise his improbable moves, but behind Jordan's primary defender Detroit had several extremely big players—Bill Laimbeer and James Edwards—with whom it clogged the lane, as well as shot blockers John Salley and Dennis Rodman to help out. The idea was to use Jordan's confidence and willingness to rise to a challenge—he would go to the hoop against anyone, no matter how big, and Bach marveled at his ability to attack double teams by going through or over them, not, as did other players, by passing the ball—against him by encouraging him to work the middle, where he would find an extremely rough road to the basket.

The most fundamental tenet of the Jordan Rules—that two players needed to guard him each time he touched the ball—would seem to have been most obvious, but there were coaches around the league who insisted on checking him with a single player. For the most part, they paid a terrible price. Cleveland Cavaliers' coach Lenny Wilkens, for in-

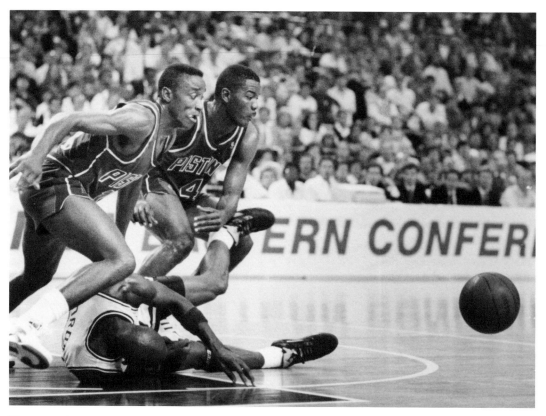

Thomas and Dumars pursue a loose ball over a prone Jordan. Though the Pistons reached the NBA finals in 1988, 1989, and 1990 and won the championship the latter two of those years, their punishing style of play earned them much criticism.

stance, preferred to commit just one of his defenders at a time to the care of Jordan, and his Cavaliers had been eliminated from the playoffs for two years running by the Bulls; in the 1988 playoff series Jordan had averaged an otherworldly 45 points a game against Cleveland, and in a contest during the just completed regular season he lit up the Cavaliers for 69 points.

Yet basketball analysts rightly pointed out that it was the personnel Daly had available to enact the Jordan Rules that was as much responsible for their success as the concepts they embodied. Jordan's primary one-on-one defender, the Detroit guard Joe Dumars, was, aside from his counterpart, the league's best defensive guard. Dumars was tireless, stoic, and willing to sacrifice his offensive game by exhausting most of his energies in the thankless pursuit of guarding Jordan. The Detroit forward Dennis Rodman, who sometimes spelled Dumars in a head-up matchup with the scoring champion, was also one of the league's most accomplished defenders, and he was the rare player of his size—six feet eight inches—with the necessary quickness to stay with Jordan. The rest of Detroit's players concentrated on stopping Jordan with a single-mindedness that no other team in the league could match, and they were willing to take extraordinary measures to hold him in check. The coach of the Utah Jazz, Frank Layden, felt that all the analysis of Detroit's personnel and strategy ignored the most crucial aspect of the Pistons' approach. "The Jordan Rules?" said Layden. "You know what the Jordan rule is, don't you? Knock him on his ass. They [Detroit] can talk all they want, but the one thing they did—when he got in midair—they knocked him down."

Such tactics only aggravated the bad blood that existed between the two teams, which by 1990 had made their rivalry the most bitter in the league. Jordan felt that the Pistons, especially their thuggish center Bill Laimbeer, consistently—and intentionally—crossed the line that separates aggressive from dirty and dangerous play, and he believed that Detroit's intent was to injure him as much as it was to stop him. That Detroit had successfully used such tactics to claim the gaudy bauble that so many said would be the ultimate and only true validation of Jordan's greatness—the NBA championship ring—only magnified the intensity of his dislike of the Pistons.

Moreover, Jordan and Detroit's best player, the wondrous little point guard Isiah Thomas, harbored a deep animosity for one another. Thomas had resented the Bulls player's fame and fortune since Jordan's entrance into the league, especially because it had been achieved in his hometown of Chicago and at the expense of some of his own commercial endorsements, and he had allegedly gone so far as to organize a "freeze-out" of Jordan in the 1985 All-Star Game. (At Thomas's instigation, several of Jordan's teammates on the Eastern Conference squad had refused to pass him the ball.)

The Pistons were also not above taunting Jordan for the alleged selfishness of his play. "There's not one guy who sets the tone on our team. That's what makes us a team," John Salley told reporters on the eve of the 1990 confrontation with Chicago. "If one guy did everything, we wouldn't be a team; we'd be the Chicago Bulls. We don't care who scores the points as long as we win. It would be hard for Michael Jordan to play on this team because he's got to score

Jordan and Thomas enjoy a rare moment of on-court friendliness; their dislike for one another was usually much less well concealed. Though the frequent subject of negative publicity, the diminutive Thomas was one of the NBA's most remarkable and entertaining performers, an explosive scorer and magical passer who by the late 1980s had succeeded in blending his own extraordinary individual skills with those of his teammates to make the Pistons champions.

all the points. I don't think he'd fit in here." Though the Pistons were the most successful team in the league, not one of their players ranked in the top ten in any offensive category.

Such comments only fed Jordan's determination to silence his critics forever, and there was no doubt that, for all Detroit's success against his team, 1990 constituted his best chance to date. He entered the Eastern Conference Finals on a roll, having just played, in the course of Chicago's five-game victory over the Philadelphia 76ers, what he described as the best four consecutive games of his life. Over the course of the Philadelphia series, he had averaged a phenomenal 43 points per game on 55 percent shooting and had also contributed 7 rebounds and 7 assists per contest.

The Bulls and their fans shared a certainty that if they got by Detroit, the championship ring that Jordan desired so desperately would be theirs. As John Bach put it, "There's always been a feeling on this team that if we got to the Finals, Michael would figure out how to win it. He's the greatest competitor I've ever seen, and then he goes to still another level in the big games." Though Chicago's past record against Detroit gave little reason for optimism, they had faced a similar situation in the playoffs the previous year, when they were matched up with a Cleveland team that had beaten them six straight times in the regular season. Jordan had publicly promised that the Bulls would win anyway, and they had, ousting the Cavaliers in the last second of the deciding game. (The winning basket, of course, had been scored by Jordan—an 18-foot, hanging, floating, double-pump jumper, under defensive pressure so intense that he never even saw the ball nestle into the hoop, that came after he overruled his coach's decision to set up the final shot for one of his teammates by slamming his fist down on the clipboard where the play had been drawn up and demanding, "Give me the ball.") And in 1990, Jordan brought a much more talented supporting cast with him to the conference finals, chief among them the multitalented forward Scottie Pippen, who in his third season was showing signs of fulfilling his splendid potential.

At home, Detroit easily won the first two games, 86–77 and 102–93. The Jordan Rules worked extremely well; the Pistons held their nemesis to an extremely hard-earned 27 points a game, achieved on less than 40 percent shooting. Knocked frequently to the floor, Jordan was limping on a bruised leg and hip by the close of Game 2, and his teammates, as they had the year before in the conference finals, appeared tentative and intimidated. In Game 1, Jordan's partners at guard, John Paxson and Craig Hodges, missed all of their shots; handcuffed by Rodman's defensive

Having eluded Dumars, Jordan prepares to elevate. "I basically know I am going to have to expend more energy in a game against Michael Jordan than against anybody else," Dumars has said. "You tell yourself that you can't get tired, because if you do, he senses any kind of letup and then there will be an explosion from him."

work, Pippen confessed to spending "too much time worrying about how he's going to play me." With his team trailing by 15 points at halftime of Game 2, Jordan stormed into the locker room, threw a chair, and cursed his teammates for their timidity. After the game, Jordan, who was at most times unusually cooperative with the press, refused to speak with reporters, leaving his teammates to comment on the game. "I'll let them stand up and take responsibility for themselves," he said to a friend.

The next day at practice, he was equally surly at what he regarded as his teammates' lack of seriousness. "I looked over and saw Horace [Grant] and Scottie screwing around, joking and messing up," Jordan was quoted as saying to a friend by Chicago newspaperman Sam Smith. "They've got the talent, but they don't take it seriously. And the rookies were together, as usual. They've got no idea what it's all about. The white guys, they work hard, but they don't have the talent. And the rest of them? Who knows what to expect? They're not much good for anything." To his fellow Bulls and the media, the General, as Jordan's teammates sometimes referred to him, remained silent.

Halftime of Game 3 saw Chicago trailing by eight points, but in the third and fourth quarters Jordan abandoned his efforts to get his teammates more involved—he had taken, for him, a low total of just 43 shots in the first two games—and poured in 31 points, 18 of them in the fourth quarter, as the Bulls, in front of a characteristically raucous crowd at Chicago Stadium, rallied for a five-point victory. "Tonight we showed that it wasn't the rules against Jordan but that Jordan rules," crowed the jubilant Chicago coach, Phil Jackson, after the game. Jordan finished with 47 points and 10 rebounds, while Pippen contributed 29 points and 11 boards. The next game followed a similar pattern, with the Bulls coming from behind, sparked by Jordan's 42 points, for a seven-point victory. For the first time in two years, Detroit had lost two playoff games in a row; of their five playoff losses over that same span (against 24 wins), four had been to Chicago.

But the Bad Boys were back, in front of their home crowd, for Game 5. Shadowed relentlessly by Dumars and his cohorts, Jordan shot an abysmal 7 for

Not high enough: Rodman gets off a shot over the outstretched arms of Jordan and Horace Grant in Game 3 of the 1990 Eastern Conference Finals.

19. Pippen, who was slammed brutally to the floor by Thomas on a drive, shot even worse—5 for 20. In desperate need of a breather, Jordan left the floor for just two minutes in the third quarter, and during that brief span the Pistons outscored the Bulls by 9 points. Detroit won by 14, but Chicago, on the brink of elimination, rallied to route the Pistons by 18 points in Game 6, with Jordan tossing in 18 points in the crucial third quarter, when the Bulls blew the game open to tie the Pistons at three games apiece.

The season—and Jordan's quest—had come down to a single game. Chicago held a two-point lead early in the second half, then fell apart as Jordan's teammates, in basketball parlance, "disappeared." Scottie Pippen scored just one basket in 10 attempts, for a total of two points; though he pled the excuse of a migraine, observers, Jordan among them, remembered that he had retreated to the bench early in Game 7 against the Pistons the previous year with a concussion and wondered whether he had the heart to perform well in crucial games. Horace Grant shot 3 for 17, rookie B. J. Armstrong shot 1 for 8, and Craig Hodges made just 3 of 13 shots. Though Jordan scored or assisted on every Chicago basket of the second half until he left the game, he could not do it alone, and the Bulls went down to a devastating 93–74 defeat. Though Jordan had shot just 47 percent from the floor—below average for him, but still exceptional against Detroit's unyielding defense—his teammates had been positively atrocious, shooting a horrific 38 percent. "They may have the best player, but we have the better team," chortled Laimbeer amid the celebration in the Pistons' locker room.

Across the way, in the somber Chicago locker room, Pippen sat sobbing, his head cradled in his huge hands. "We have to do some things. We have to make some changes," Jordan said. ◖◗

2
"ONE DAY GOD MADE THE PERFECT BASKETBALL PLAYER"

Jordan at bat as a 12-year-old in his hometown of Wilmington, North Carolina. As a youth, Jordan preferred baseball to basketball.

MICHAEL JORDAN WAS the fourth child—there would ultimately be five: James Ronald, Deloris, Larry, Michael, and Roslyn—and the third and last son born to James and Deloris Jordan. Though he considers himself a native of North Carolina, and though both of the older Jordans were natives of small rural towns in that state, Michael was actually born in another hoops hotbed—Brooklyn, New York. The growing family had come north with James, who, ambitious for a better life for his wife and offspring, was attending a vocational school in New York City run by General Electric, his employer back home in Wallace, North Carolina.

The move had not been an easy one for Deloris Jordan, who was pregnant, responsible for the care of three small children, and also working a full-time job. Her situation became even more difficult toward the end of 1962 with the news that her beloved mother had suddenly died, and when the combination of stress and sorrow began to endanger her pregnancy, her doctors recommended that she take to her bed for the duration of her term. She complied for a week, then, with little real choice in the matter, resumed her myriad responsibilities. Consequently, there was great concern that Deloris's hardship would affect the health and well-being of the infant who would enter the world on February 17, 1963, as Michael Jeffrey Jordan. "The near miscarriage was very bad," James Jordan later remembered. "When Michael was born, we thought there might be something wrong with him. He was born with a nosebleed. The hospital kept him three days after Deloris was discharged. He'd have nosebleeds for no reason until he was five years old."

For his mother, the birth of the child she had come so close to losing was a special, even blessed, event. Deloris says "that Michael's birth was like a sign. I lost my mother unexpectedly while carrying Michael, and he was my godsend. Michael was the happiness He sent me after a very sad time in my life."

As it is for most parents, that happiness was mixed with worry, even though their newborn was merry and easygoing and content to amuse himself. "He was such a jolly baby. He never cried. Just feed him and give him something to play with and he was fine," his mother remembered. But there were the nosebleeds, and one time baby Michael managed to wriggle himself off the edge of the bed and become trapped between it and the wall, where he nearly suffocated.

The Jordans' youngest son was a born charmer, with a mischievous streak that seemed to prompt him to court danger and a lucky star that enabled him always to walk away unharmed, emboldened by his good fortune to test the fates once again in the not-far-off future. At age two or so, he watched with fascination one evening as his father went about preparing to do some maintenance work on the family automobile in the backyard of James Jordan's parents' home in Wallace. (The Jordans had returned to North Carolina as soon as James had completed his coursework in New York City.) Needing a trouble light to illuminate the engine, James had run a series of frayed extension cords along the ground, which was still soaked from recent heavy rains, from the house to the automobile. As he leaned over the engine, he noticed some movement out of the corner of his eye and turned to see his curious youngest son bending down to pick up the cords at the point where they were joined together. The jolt from the un-grounded cords threw the little boy three feet back-ward through the air before his father even had time to shout. "I've thought to myself since, My God, how this world would've been cheated if the cord had gotten tangled up with Michael and not let him go," James Jordan said many years afterward. "He would've been electrocuted."

Undeterred by his premature experience in auto-motive repair, at the age of five Michael decided to help his parents out by chopping some wood, despite their prohibition on his using the axe. To make matters worse, he decided to take his first lesson in woodcutting while barefoot. (Like many country children, young Michael customarily ran around out-doors without shoes.) "So I'm chopping little bits and pieces of wood," Jordan told a television interviewer years later, "and being hardheaded, and I accidentally missed the wood and caught half of my big toe." His parents rushed the screaming child to the house of a neighbor, who was reputed to have some knowledge of first aid. The neighbor doused the injured digit in kerosene, which killed the pain. No permanent dam-age was incurred, though Jordan is fond of relating that "every time I fall now my father keeps telling me, 'You shouldn't have played with that ax.'"

Though mischief and accidents were a common part of Michael Jordan's childhood, his desire to help his parents with their work was an anomaly. "Michael was probably the laziest kid I had," his father remembered to Bob Sakamoto, one of Jordan's biographers. "He would give every last dime of his allowance to his brothers and sisters and even kids in the neighborhood to do his chores. . . . That really got me."

Avoidance of hard work was not something that either James or Deloris Jordan would readily tolerate. The son of a sharecropper, James Jordan grew up on a farm outside of Wallace, and by the age of 10 he was already driving a tractor. "I grew up on a farm without the luxuries a lot of kids have," he remembered. "I came from a small farming town. If one family owned a television, the other 10 families would come over to watch it. There were farm chores, and when I was 17, I drove a school bus part-time." After high school, James Jordan joined the air force; after finishing his stint in the service, he returned to Wallace to marry Deloris and take a job with General Electric, where he worked his way up from forklift operator to dispatcher and finally, before retiring to look after some of his third son's business affairs, to supervisor. His wife was also no stranger to hard work; after raising five children, Deloris Jordan took a job at the drive-through window for United Carolina Bank. In a short time she was promoted to head teller and then director of customer service.

Though Michael now sees aspects of both his parents in himself—"my personality and my laughter come from my father; my business and serious side come from my mother"—James and Deloris Jordan experienced a certain amount of frustration in shaping his character. Although he did not always channel it in ways that his parents found constructive, Michael possessed an exceptionally strong will, and he was not afraid to test it. "If there was something to be tried, he was the one to try it. If someone needed to be disciplined more, he was the one who needed it. He was going to test you to the end," his mother

Michael's parents, Deloris and James Jordan. "Everything starts with them," Jordan says. According to his friend Fred Whitfield, "If you look at the reasons that Michael has been so successful, one is the values he learned from his parents."

has said. His father also remembers that his fourth child was "always testing us," often by purposely "messing up" his chores. "If we told him the stove was hot, don't touch, he'd touch it. If there was a wet-paint sign, he'd touch the paint to see if it was wet."

"I was lazy about some things," Jordan has said about his childhood. "I never got into mowing the lawn or doing hard jobs." Each year during the harvest, his brothers and sisters worked part-time cutting tobacco, but when Michael tried it, he quit after the first day, claiming that his back hurt. Likewise, when his mother got him a job one summer as a maintenance worker in a hotel, he lasted only a few days. "I just couldn't do it," he said recently. "I could not keep regular hours. It just wasn't me."

Jordan was then in high school; aside from playing professional basketball, his brief employment in the hotel is the only job he has ever held. "If you hand him a wrench, he wouldn't know what to turn with it," his mother has said. "If he had to get a job in a factory punching a clock, he'd starve to death," claims his father.

The area where Michael finally focused his willfulness and abundant energy was sports. All of the Jordan children were athletes, and Michael competed regularly against his older brothers and their friends, especially once the family, in 1970, moved to Wilmington, a small city on the Atlantic Ocean in southeast North Carolina, where James fashioned a basketball court in the backyard of the family home. The court soon became something of a neighborhood hangout.

"We'd have every kid in the neighborhood at our house in Wilmington because it was the only one with a basketball court," Bob Sakamoto quoted James Jordan as saying in 1991. "There would be 20 guys over between the ages of 10 and 18. That's how Michael learned how to play. We were almost like a park. Deloris would buy 15 pounds of hot dogs and hamburgers and we'd make a picnic out of it."

Michael's fiercest rival in those days was his brother Larry, who was a year older. An exceptionally talented player who was denied a celebrated basketball career of his own only because he stopped growing at a height of five feet eight inches, Larry Jordan was reputedly an even better leaper than his younger sibling is today, and fistfights often spiced their spirited backyard one-on-one contests. "Those backyard games really helped me become the player that I am in a lot of ways," Jordan says today. "Larry would never give me any slack, never took it easy on me. He'd rather beat me up than have me beat him in a game. I learned a lot about being competitive from him." Until Michael's sophomore year at Laney High School in Wilmington, Larry almost always won their games, but that year Michael sprouted up to five feet eleven. He would grow almost five more inches in his remaining three years of high school, and his older brother's backyard dominance was forever ended. "Oh yeah, I used to be able to take him most of the time," Larry told Sakamoto, "but once he started shooting up and getting taller, I had more problems staying with him."

Initially, however, baseball, not basketball, was Jordan's favorite sport. According to Bob Billingsly, his coach at D.C. Virgo Junior High School, this made Jordan somewhat unusual. In Wilmington, as elsewhere in the South during the years when Jordan was growing up, legal segregation was waning, but a profusion of unwritten racial codes still held sway. Among these was the notion that basketball was a black man's game, while baseball was for whites. According to Billingsly, the Babe Ruth baseball field was in a white part of town where many blacks were afraid to travel, and Jordan was one of the few black children to stay with the sport all the way through junior high. "He had a real love-hate thing with the white kids," Billingsly told Jim Naughton, author of *Taking to the Air: The Rise of Michael Jordan*. "He got along with them, but he wasn't afraid to stand up for himself. He didn't take anything from them."

Jordan as a student at D.C. Virgo Junior High School.

And it was as a baseball player that Jordan first drew notice for his athletic prowess. "The way he played baseball in Little League, he made me become a fan," recalled James Jordan, who much preferred his son's work on the diamond to his backyard efforts to emulate stuntman Evel Knievel on a small motorbike he had somehow obtained. "If I wouldn't take him to play ball, he'd look so pitiful, like he'd lost every friend in the world and was all by himself. You'd take one look at him and say, 'Okay, let's go.' He would

Like many a teenager, Jordan confessed to feeling "goony" as an adolescent, but his yearbook photo (right) from Laney High School reveals a poised, handsome young man.

do things in baseball and excel beyond kids his age that you would just get caught up in it."

To this day, Jordan considers the state baseball championship he won with his Babe Ruth League team his greatest accomplishment. "My favorite childhood memory, my greatest accomplishment," he told sportswriter Sam Smith, author of *The Jordan Rules*, a chronicle of his 1990–91 NBA season, "was when I got the Most Valuable Player award when my team won the state baseball championship. That was the first thing I accomplished in my life, and you always remember the first. I remember I batted over .500, hit five home runs in seven games, and pitched a one-hitter to get us into the championship game."

Just as Michael's baseball exploits demonstrated to his father unimagined capacities and abilities on

the part of his "lazy" and willful son, his success on the ballfield contributed immeasurably to his own self-esteem. Like most adolescents, Michael was sensitive about his appearance, and with his protruding ears and "little boy's haircut" (an extremely close cropped style), he considered himself "goony-looking." His unflattering nickname was Bald Head. "I'd look in the mirror and feel I was ugly. A lot of guys," he said years later, "picked on me, and they would do it in front of the girls. They would joke about my haircut and the way I played with my tongue out and just different things. And the girls would, kind of, they would laugh at that, and right then, I was dead. I couldn't get a date with anybody." On the baseball diamond, he was able to draw a more positive kind of attention to himself.

A potentially greater source of damage to Jordan's self-esteem were the various attitudes, conditions, and practices in the South that, even after the end of legal segregation, often combined to make blacks—politically, economically, and socially—second-class citizens. Though both James and Deloris Jordan had grown up under segregation, both raised their children to ignore the question of race as much as possible—both as a barrier to achievement or as a means of judging people.

A talented basketball player himself when in high school, James had seen his own athletic opportunities limited by segregation: "At least half of our high school games were played on outdoor courts because our school couldn't afford an indoor gym. . . . Black schools only played black schools and never got any exposure like kids get now." Yet in the day-to-day life of his family, James found common ground with whites in the poverty the two groups shared: "I grew up in a neighborhood where everyone was poor, black and white. We were forced to share by nature. . . . We all worked in the fields together, black and white. . . . Deloris and I grew up among whites and got along. It's not really what color you are, it's who you are. It's not what you amass or what you have that makes you different, it's your personality. You can have the

Jordan had to wait longer than he wanted to don the uniform of the Laney High varsity, for as a sophomore he was cut from the team. The slight only made him focus more intently on his game.

most money in the world and still be a jerk. You can have no money at all and be the nicest man in the world. People like you for what you are, those are your real friends. We made sure they understood that lesson. None of my kids was ever touched by segregation." Deloris Jordan preached a similar message to her children. "You just didn't judge people's color. Even if people were ignorant and said racial things, you just looked beyond that. Either you could let it affect you or you could struggle against it and move on. And that's what I did."

Though not untouched by prejudice—he was suspended in the ninth grade for squashing a popsicle in the hair of a girl who called him a nigger—Michael seemed to take his parents' lessons seriously. Among his many friends—of her children, Deloris said, Michael was the "one who liked people more"—were both black and white children. He says today that "the greatest lesson" he learned from his parents "is that I never see you for the color. I see you for the person you are. I know I'm recognized as being black, but I don't look at you as black or white, just as a person."

By the time Jordan entered new, integrated Laney High School as a 10th grader, basketball had replaced baseball as his primary athletic interest. As he grew taller, Michael discovered that he had gained another attribute as well—he could jump higher than any player in the area, with the possible exception of his brother Larry. His father soon grew accustomed to seeing Michael on the backyard court earnestly emulating the extraordinary moves of the North Carolina State University star David Thompson, a high-flying aerialist known as the Skywalker.

Even so, when Jordan tried out for the Laney varsity team as a sophomore, he was cut by Coach Fred Lynch in favor of a much taller player. Years later, the pain Jordan felt at the time was still palpable. "I'll never forgot how hurt I was when I saw the list posted in the hall. I cried. I was [so angry]. I couldn't cheer them on. I wanted them to lose, to prove they made a mistake. I think, to be successful, you have to be selfish."

James Jordan came to regard the cut as a good thing in the long run in that it forced his perhaps too naturally gifted son to focus on basketball a seriousness equal to his evident and prodigious talent. Now, for the first time, Michael Jordan began not just to play basketball, but to work on his game—and with a single-minded intensity. "I've got to believe one thing," his father said many years later. "One day, God was sitting around and decided to make Himself the perfect basketball player. He gave him a little hardship early in life to make him appreciate what he would earn in the end, and called him Michael Jordan."

3

THE SHOT

Aside from the ultimate source of his unusual abilities, the essential mystery of Michael Jordan's career has been why such an incandescent talent failed initially to impress the full measure of his brilliance upon so many observers. After being cut from the varsity, Jordan played for the Laney High junior varsity team, for which he averaged 25 points a game. He began as well a daily regimen of six A.M. training and practice sessions, designed to ensure that he would never again have to endure the humiliation of being cut from a team. As a junior and senior on the varsity team, he went on to average more than 20 points a game, yet he still was not regarded as a particularly outstanding talent, especially in a state that prides itself on the exceptional quality of its high school and college ball. Unlike his future contemporaries in the NBA Magic Johnson and Isiah Thomas, who began receiving feelers from college recruiters while they were still in junior high school, Jordan was not much sought after by the nation's universities and colleges. He failed to make a widely circulated list of the nation's top 300 basketball prospects and had to make his own overtures of interest to such college basketball powerhouses as the University of Virginia

Rising to the occasion: Jordan soars to the rim as a freshman at the University of North Carolina. The team's upperclassmen voted Jordan cockiest freshman, but by the end of the season he had fully justified his self-confidence.

and the University of California at Los Angeles, both of which ignored him. Aware that no player from Wilmington had enjoyed success at a major college basketball program, Michael's counselors at Laney urged him to consider attending a service academy or a Division III school. (Division III is the lowest level of intercollegiate competion; its constituent schools award no athletic scholarships.)

Nor was Jordan in much demand at the many summer basketball camps, both in his own state and around the country, that are traditionally used by college coaches as markets at which to evaluate and recruit high school talent. Years later, Bobby Cremins, head basketball coach at Georgia Tech and one of the most persuasive and dogged recruiters of high school talent, was flabbergasted to learn that Jordan had attended his basketball camp at Appalachian State University in North Carolina in the summer of 1980, just before his senior year at Laney. Cremins had no memory of him as a player at all.

But that same summer, at the nation's premier showcase for high school hoops talent, Howie Garfinkel's Five Star Camp in Pittsburgh, Jordan made a much greater impression. Originally, he had not even been invited to the camp because, according to longtime NBA assistant coach Brendan Malone, who was then associated with Five Star, "the only people who knew about him were in North Carolina." Roy Williams, then an assistant to Dean Smith, the legendary coach at the University of North Carolina (UNC) whose camp Jordan had attended, recommended him to the people at Five Star. Though Jordan was not invited to the first week-long session at Pittsburgh, which was reserved exclusively for those players regarded as the nation's best, he excelled at the next two sessions—he was named most valuable player for each—and for the first time attracted some serious attention. "He just steps out on the court and it's like he's playing a different game," a camp official said at the time. "It was like there were no defenders." Malone remembered that "his ability to put the ball on the floor and take it to the basket really jumped out at you." For Jordan, his two weeks at Five Star marked his first inkling of the true extent of his basketball potential. "It was as though somebody had tapped me on the shoulder with a magic wand and said, 'You must emerge as somebody—somebody to be admired, to achieve big things.'"

Tipped off by Williams about Jordan's performance, the coaching staff at UNC now began to express an interest in Jordan. What the Jordan sweepstakes lacked in numbers—"no one was recruiting him at that time," Malone remembered—it now made up for in caliber, for UNC had one of the elite college basketball programs in the country. It belonged to arguably the nation's toughest college basketball league, the Atlantic Coast Conference (ACC); its coach, Dean Smith, already regarded as possibly the country's finest, would go on to record more wins than any college coach in history; and the Tar Heels were a perennial Top Twenty team and contender for the national championship who, in their famous sky blue uniforms, appeared regularly on national television and always played before capacity crowds, at home and on the road. A large number of Tar Heel players went on to the professional ranks, where, well trained in Smith's team-oriented system, they were often even more individually outstanding than they had been in college. The North Carolina program—referred to by some, with a mixture of admiration, jealousy, and derision, as the "Carolina Corporation" or the "IBM of College Basketball"— was so successful that it was said, with a great degree of truth, that Smith did not have to recruit talent so much as simply select among the many blue-chip players clamoring to play there.

Michael's parents, particularly his mother, were delighted by North Carolina's interest. Smith had a reputation for taking a genuine interest in his players' academic progress as well as in their athletic development, and almost all of his players earned their degrees, which was important to Deloris Jordan. When she met the coach, she later recalled, "we talked education, we didn't talk basketball. He didn't come in making a lot of promises. He said, 'If you work hard and qualify academically we'll see about your coming onto our basketball team.'"

Though Michael was a solid student, with a B average, who planned on majoring in geography, such considerations were not as important to him as they were to his mother. North Carolina was a region of fierce interstate collegiate-basketball rivalries, and Jordan had grown up a fan of UNC's fiercest rival, North Carolina State, which is where he was initially interested in playing. "Growing up, I hated North Carolina. My mom liked Phil Ford [a UNC star and longtime professional standout], but I couldn't stand him or any of those UNC guys," Jordan said. But when a coaching change left Jordan uncertain about the future direction of the N.C. State program, he decided on North Carolina, where he matriculated in the fall of 1981.

Jordan's likely value to the already vaunted UNC program was made quickly apparent. On his first visit to the bucolic campus at Chapel Hill, he made a lasting impression on a freshman named Ken Stewart, who witnessed an outdoor pick-up game on a court behind his dormitory. "The first time I saw him was when he came for his visit," Stewart said. "There was a court behind the dorm. He came out doing 360s, alley-oops, slamming over people, and that was the first we had heard of him." A Tar Heel player, Darryl Summey, who took part in that game, remembered that "here was this guy doing stuff we'd never seen before and calling attention to himself."

The flamboyance of Jordan's game was his natural way of expressing himself on the court—the great jazz trumpeter Wynton Marsalis compares Jordan's creativity on the hardwood to the spontaneous improvisations of a brilliant jazz instrumentalist—but his "calling attention to himself," in the form of verbal tauntings and boasts, marked his lasting hurt at the disrespect that he felt others continued to show his game. Several years later, observers marveled at the ferocity, intense even by Jordan's standards and replete with much trash-talking, with which he savaged Adrian Branch, a scared newcomer trying to make the Chicago team, in several training-camp one-on-one matchups. Jordan, already an established NBA superstar, seemingly had nothing to prove in such a confrontation, but Branch, it turned out, had been one of several high school All-Americans who had taunted and insulted him at various camps for his relatively unheralded status as a high school player.

Jordan's boastfulness also served to mask a certain insecurity about his abilities. Once he had made his decision to attend North Carolina, a number of people in his hometown had been quick to tell him that he had made a mistake, that he would never play at so excellent a program, that he would spend four years riding the bench. "When I got here, I thought everybody was a superstar and I would be the low man," Jordan confessed. Such doubts were not apparent to his roommate, Buzz Peterson, who had become Jordan's friend when they attended several basketball camps together. "Times when we were together I'd say to myself, 'I can't live with this guy.' Sometimes I'd say, 'Why do I have to listen to this guy talk and run his mouth all the time?' When we got on the

Jordan goes baseline against one of North Carolina's rivals in the Atlantic Coast Conference (ACC), the Clemson University Tigers. "You could see him becoming more sure of himself in everything he did," teammate James Worthy said of Jordan as a freshman. "Each game he gained a little respect."

court he'd tell you, 'I'm better than you. I can do this better than you.' Sometimes you hate to hear that, but you've got to have that if you're going to be a good athlete."

And it was immediately apparent that Jordan was not just a good athlete but an extraordinary one. In the first week of practice, Smith was surprised to discover that "we didn't have anybody who could guard him," and Jordan was quickly elevated to the starting five—only the eighth freshman in Smith's long tenure to attain such elevated status. He turned the team's first game into a showcase of, as *Durham Sun* sportswriter Al Featherson put it, his "awesome skills," recording 22 points on 11 for 15 shooting and amassing four steals.

"After the first game I realized I was as good as everybody else," Jordan said, a fact that was equally apparent to his teammates. Said junior forward James Worthy, an All-American who was destined to be the first selection in the NBA draft at the close of the season: "I've never seen anybody pick up the game so fast. Michael just doesn't make mistakes." Point guard Jimmy Black was even more effusive in his praise. "Michael is everything you see of him," Black said. "He can do it all: score, play defense, lead the team, rebound, block shots. What else is there?" Atlantic Coast Conference coaches were equally impressed; at season's end, they voted Jordan the league's Freshman Player of the Year.

With Jordan adding his superlative talents to an already splendid squad anchored by Worthy and star center Sam Perkins, the Tar Heels easily claimed the Atlantic Coast Conference regular-season and tournament championship and swept through to the finals of the NCAA tournament, which determines the national collegiate champion. Their opponent in the 1982 finals, played at the Superdome in New Orleans, was Georgetown University, led by a stellar freshman of its own, center Patrick Ewing, who was making the first of his three appearances in the finals. For Smith, the game represented an opportunity to attain one of the few coaching honors that had been denied him: for all his victories, and for all the superb players he had coached there, he had not won a national championship in his 24 years at North Carolina, a fact that critics of his accomplishments were quick to point out.

The championship game was an extremely hard fought, nip-and-tuck contest from the outset. With 32 seconds remaining, North Carolina, trailing by a point at 62–61, called for a time-out. The obvious

Though perhaps everyone who has ever picked up a basketball has fantasized about winning a championship game with a last-second shot, few get the opportunity to make their dream a reality. With 17 seconds to go in the NCAA championship game and his team trailing Georgetown University by a point, Jordan releases "the shot."

play was to work the ball inside to Perkins or to the sizzling Worthy, who had already scorched the celebrated Georgetown defense for 28 points. But Smith knew that Georgetown, with the fearsome Ewing patrolling the lane, would be bracing for such an approach, and he decided—as Jordan's coaches would do so often in the years to come—to put the ball, and the game, in Jordan's hand. The final play was designed for Jordan to take the last shot. "Do it, Michael, just knock it in," the venerable coach whispered to the freshman as the teams returned to the floor.

The Tar Heels worked the ball passively around the perimeter as the game's last half-minute ticked away. Finally, with about 19 seconds left on the clock,

Jimmy Black, on the right side of the court, drew the Georgetown defenders toward him with a quick feint toward the basket and then snapped the ball all the way across the court to Jordan on the left wing. He caught the ball and went up in the same motion, elevating high off the floor and reaching the apex of his jump with 17 seconds left. His jump shot, at this stage in his career the weakest part of his game, tended normally to be flat, without much arc, but this time he unleashed "a rainbow."

In the Superdome stands, James Jordan covered his face with his hands as his son left the floor to release his shot. Next to him, Deloris screamed out a delighted expletive as the ball swished through the net, giving Carolina the lead—and the championship. With time enough to get a final shot of their own, Georgetown hurried the ball upcourt and then turned it over, returning possession to North Carolina. Seconds later, the clock ran out, and the Tar Heels were the national champions.

"That's when everything started," Jordan would say later about what Tar Heel fans usually refer to simply as "the shot." "That's when Michael Jordan started to get his respect." ◀◉▶

4

PLAYER OF THE YEARS

◈

ALONG WITH THE respect and celebrity that
Michael Jordan gained as a result of "the shot"—re-
plays of the basket were shown constantly on highlight reels and as part of the NCAA's promotion of
"March Madness," as it referred to its annual spring-
time tournament, and, among other tokens of burgeoning fame, the 19-year-old hero was featured on
the cover of the Chapel Hill telephone book—came
an increased devotion to improving his game.

Jordan had by now become the quintessential gym
rat; two days after the season ended, he was back in
North Carolina's Woollen Gymnasium, participating
in pick-up games against anyone willing to take him
on. These sessions, which continued morning, after-
noon, and night throughout the summer of 1982,
have become something of a legend in UNC lore, for
Jordan's challengers included, among current Tar
Heel players and hopeful newcomers, some of the
most distinguished hoops alumni the university had
produced, including several professional players. Yet
Jordan dominated virtually every contest. "It was
always expected," said Ken Stewart, a regular witness,
"that his team would win every game if it had any
help at all." Carolina player Darryl Summey recalled

*In 1984, Jordan brought his
flawless form to the NBA, where
he was immediately an even more
dominant player than he had been
in college.*

57

in conversation with Jim Naughton that Jordan "took on everybody. Al Wood, Dudley Bradley [former Tar Heel standouts gone on to the professional ranks]. Bradley was supposed to be a defensive ace, but Michael took him outside and then took him inside. He could pretty much do what he wanted in those games. He just about had carte blanche."

To North Carolina sports information director Rick Brewer, who had seen several generations of Tar Heel players, the shot did not make that much of a difference in Jordan's development, but others disagreed. According to Brewer, "The shot didn't change him that much. He was a vastly improved player his sophomore year, but most coaches believe that's when a player makes his biggest strides. Maybe that shot did give him a little boost, a little more confidence. A lot of people claim he really didn't know what he was doing when he took that shot."

To other observers, it was clear that Jordan's success in the truest test of basketball mettle—the waning seconds of a close championship game—had transformed him, thrust upon him for perhaps the first time a genuine understanding of the full extent of his gifts and made him a player of true inner confidence as well as outward bravado. According to his roommate and close friend Buzz Peterson, "After [the shot] his confidence just shot up and he just grew." Perhaps more than anyone else, Peterson was in the best position to appreciate—although not without a certain amount of regret—Jordan's startling development at North Carolina. As a high school senior in Asheville, North Carolina, Peterson had been voted the North Carolina High School Player of the Year, and he was considered a much more promising college prospect than Jordan. When the two—both of whom played off, or shooting, guard—became such good friends that they agreed to attend the same college, Peterson never suspected that he would wind up riding the Carolina bench behind Jordan. "Here I was committing to a school with a guy who played the same position as me," Peterson said years later. "I guess you could say it wasn't a good decision in terms of playing time. I mean, I knew he was pretty good, but I didn't think he was going to be that good."

Another observer in a position to make a meaningful evaluation of Jordan's progress was Coach Dean Smith. The difference between the surprisingly accomplished freshman and the player who emerged from Woollen Gym in the late autumn of 1982 to begin practice with the Tar Heels was, in Smith's words, like "night and day."

The coach noted improvement in virtually every aspect of the prodigy's game—"defense, confidence, rebounding, position, passing, ball handling"—failing to mention only that area in which Jordan was already so accomplished as to make further development seem almost excessive: his offense. Revealing themselves ever more frequently now were the characteristic explosive, slithering drives in which it seemed that Jordan, tongue dangling from his open mouth over his lower lip, juking and feinting with head and shoulders and eyes and seemingly every part of his body, changed directions a dozen times in the course of negotiating a scant 15 feet of hardwood before soaring above and around his earthbound guardians to slam the ball through the hoop with either hand, or, in more difficult circumstances (harried perhaps by a trio of much taller men determinedly protecting their basket), similarly ambidextrous, to flip it gently and accurately off the glass with an instantly calibrated and proper amount of spin as he descended to the floor or, again, less ambitious but no less determined, to halt his quickest rush to the rim with a squeak of rubber soles against the wood floor as his earnest but overmatched defender reels backward and he rises, ball cradled in his right hand above and in front of his head, balanced by his left, to hang suspended for a brief eternity while all others fall to earth and he at last releases his only gently arcing, soft jump shot. Grown now to his full height of six feet six inches, Jordan was in the process of becoming the greatest offensive machine the game would ever know.

Weakened by the departure of Worthy to the NBA, North Carolina was nevertheless still a formidable squad. Though the Tar Heels could not duplicate their national-championship form of the previous year, their 1982–83 season was not without its accomplishments. The highlight of the season was undoubtedly the February 10, 1983, showdown with ACC rival the University of Virginia, which was then ranked first in the nation's polls. Anchored by its agile 7-foot, 4-inch center, Ralph Sampson, Virginia took a 16-point lead with nine minutes to go.

But behind Jordan's ball-hawking defense and uncanny offense, the Tar Heels halved the lead at the four-minute mark and then cut it to three with a little over a minute remaining. A missed Carolina jump shot seemed to mark the end of the Tar Heel comeback, but Jordan rocketed off the floor and floated above the towering Sampson to tip the rebound back into the basket. Knees crouched, body low, hands poised, snakelike, to strike, eyes darting back and forth between the ball and the man he was assigned to guard, Jordan stalked Virginia's guards as they moved up court. Foolishly, a Virginia ball handler allowed him within striking range; in an instant the ball, and the game, and the Cavaliers' top ranking were gone. Jordan lashed out, flicked the ball away, pursued and controlled it, and jetted away from the nine other men on the court toward his own hoop, where with less than a minute to play he dunked the game-winning basket.

The steal against Virginia was indicative of the single greatest improvement Jordan had made in his play: his defense. Possessed of all the physical attributes needed to be an outstanding defender—quickness, agility, and strength—Jordan now added to them the mental facets necessary to excel on his opponents' end of the floor—concentration and a willingness and determination to shut down the man he was guarding. Like most of the game's top coaches, Smith emphasized defense as the fundamental most essential to team success, and as a sophomore Jordan won Carolina's highly coveted defensive player of the game award 12 times. (He had not won it once as a freshman.)

This new focus was sorely needed, for without Worthy, North Carolina was not as highly powered an offensive unit. Though they shared the ACC regular-season conference title, the Tar Heels were upset in the conference tournament by intrastate rival N.C. State, and they lost in the third round of the NCAA tournament to an inferior Georgia squad.

For Jordan personally, however, the season was an unqualified triumph, summed up most succinctly by Al Featherson of the *Durham Sun*: "North Carolina's amazing sophomore swingman can't hide behind Dean Smith's team concept any longer. Quite simply he's become the best all-around player in college basketball. Jordan is the most talented player North Carolina or the ACC has ever seen." Curry Kirkpatrick of *Sports Illustrated* went even further, proclaiming Jordan as "merely the finest all-around amateur player in the world." The *Sporting News* settled for naming him the College Player of the Year, and professional scouts and talent evaluators began assessing his likely impact on the NBA. For at least one observer, former high-scoring guard Jeff Mullins, Jordan's professional success was more than assured: "The prevailing opinion always has been that Oscar

Robertson and Jerry West are the two best all-time guards. But we may have to change that view because of Jordan."

After leading a team of collegiate stars representing the United States to a gold medal in the Pan-American Games in Caracas, Venezuela, in the summer of 1983, Jordan returned to Chapel Hill for his junior year energized. He and everyone else concerned were expecting great things from the Tar Heels in the 1983–84 season. With point guard Kenny Smith and center Brad Daugherty—both of whom would ultimately attain All-American status and go on to star in the professional ranks—ready to play a major role alongside All-American forward Sam Perkins and player of the year Jordan, the Tar Heels were the overwhelming preseason choice of most pundits to win the national championship.

With Jordan playing the most well-rounded ball of his career and compiling a conference-leading 19.6 points per game on an excellent 55 percent from the floor, Carolina swept through the regular season, going undefeated in the conference, losing just one game overall (by one point), and maintaining the number one spot in the polls for most of the campaign. But the Tar Heels faltered in the postseason tournaments, losing first to Duke in the ACC semifinals and then to an unheralded Indiana team in the regional semifinals of the NCAA when a mediocre but grimly determined Hoosier player named Dan Dakich hounded Jordan into his poorest game of the season. Afterward, Dakich said that when his coach, the famed Bobby Knight, had given him his defensive assignment on the day before the game, "I promptly went to my room and threw up."

For Jordan, who won several more college player of the year awards, the loss to Indiana marked the end of his college career. On May 5, 1984, against the advice of his mother, who found his newfound superstardom too sudden to be completely trust-worthy and wanted him to finish his education, but with the blessing of his father and Coach Smith, Jordan announced that he would forgo his senior year at North Carolina in favor of a professional career. A little more than six weeks later, he was taken by the Chicago Bulls as the third player selected in the annual professional draft of collegiate players, behind Hakeem Olajuwon, who was chosen first by the Houston Rockets, and Sam Bowie, who was chosen second by the Portland Trailblazers. Though neither Olajuwon nor the often-injured Bowie had accomplished what Jordan had in his college career, both were much taller than he and played center, and conventional basketball wisdom held that a "big man" was the necessary first building block of a championship NBA team.

Height was not the only reason Jordan was not the first college player selected in the 1984 draft. Despite the steady brilliance of his play at North Carolina, his star had never been allowed to shine as brightly as it might have, in part because the college game, with its zone defenses, slower pace, and different style of officiating, placed less of an emphasis on quickness and the ability to put the ball on the floor and break down an individual defender with the dribble—precisely the areas where Jordan most excelled—than did the professional game, and simply because Coach Smith's celebrated system relentlessly subjugated individual interests to those of the team. Smith coached a sophisticated, structured offense that placed a premium on passing, moving without the ball, and picks. In Smith's system, for the most part, all players, no matter how talented, took advantage of scoring opportunities as they arose from the structure of the offense rather than trying to create them individually, a style that was somewhat less than congenial to Jordan's own. Although Jordan

Jordan's last performance as an amateur was as a member of the United States basketball team that won the gold medal at the 1984 Summer Olympic Games in Los Angeles, California, where his airborne excursions even won over such a staunch fundamentalist as his coach, Bobby Knight.

The untested rookie going head-to-head with the proven veteran is an eternal ritual of NBA training camps. On this October day in the Bulls's camp in 1984, newcomer Michael Jordan tested his stuff against veteran forward Orlando Woolridge, who would soon be singing the neophyte's praises.

obviously excelled under Smith—and, like most former Tar Heels, still reveres the coach—he never, at Carolina, had a true opportunity to reveal the full splendor of his individual genius, to show all that he was capable of doing. Indeed, after Jordan had begun to perform his miraculous scoring feats in the NBA, Dean Smith was the punch line to a widely circulated joke that asked who is the only man to hold Michael Jordan under 20 points a game. (Jordan averaged 17.7 points a game in his three years at North Carolina.)

The result was that at the time of the NBA draft, incomprehensible as it seems, there were still many who underestimated Jordan's abilities. According to Brendan Malone, who as an assistant coach with the Detroit Pistons would be instrumental in formulating the Jordan Rules, "Nobody, I don't care who they are, thought he would develop into a superstar. Everybody thought he'd be a good player, a very good player in [the NBA], but not to the point where you'd say he's the best one-on-one player who ever played the game." Even Jordan's close friend Fred Whitfield did not expect him to be a dominant NBA player. Whitfield "figured he would do okay. Fifteen to 17 points [per game], because he didn't score more than that in college. . . . he never handled the ball that much. He was kind of in between being a guard and being a forward."

Before Jordan began proving his doubters wrong as a professional, he had one last feat to accomplish as an amateur. In the summer of 1984, he starred as a member of the U.S. basketball team that claimed the gold medal at the Summer Olympic Games in Los Angeles. Although the Soviet Union, which to that point had fielded the only team to ever edge out the United States for a basketball gold medal, boycotted the games that year, it is doubtful that its presence would have made any difference in the outcome, for the U.S. squad, which included, among others, future professional stars Patrick Ewing and Chris Mullin in addition to Jordan, was one of the strongest such aggregations ever assembled. The United States won all its games, by an average of 32 points a game, with Jordan the most impressive of its many stars. Fernando Martin of Spain summed up the prevailing impression of Jordan gathered by his international opponents: "Michael Jordan? Jump, jump, jump. Very quick. Very fast. Jump, jump, jump."

The Olympic Games marked Jordan's second significant encounter in 1984 with Bobby Knight, who coached the U.S. squad. Many wondered how Jordan would fare under the direction of Knight, who is generally regarded as the strictest, most demanding, hardest driving, most profane coach in the game, but Knight quickly recognized the enormity of Jordan's talent and allowed him to do things his own way.

Jordan flips a semi-hook shot over center Hakeem Olajuwon of the Houston Rockets. Though Olajuwon was the first selection in the same draft in which Jordan was taken third, the Chicago newcomer wound up winning the Rookie of the Year Award.

Like talented individuals in many fields, Jordan's abilities allow him to achieve results through methods that are not always fundamentally "correct." Knight is a supreme stickler for fundamentals, but he understood that to insist that Jordan do everything by the book, exactly the way lesser players were drilled to play, would be to stifle the creativity that allowed him to do so many things that others could not. For example, players are always schooled never to "leave their feet"—to jump in the air—with the ball without knowing for certain if they are going to shoot or pass, and if the latter, to whom. But Jordan, justifiably confident in his leaping and ability to improvise a solution, consistently violates this dictum. "If I thought about a move, I'd probably turn the ball over," he has said. "I just look at a situation in the air, adjust, create and let instinct take over."

For most coaches, such an approach is anathema, justifiable only by extraordinary results. To Phil Jackson, for example, who would be the most successful of Jordan's professional coaches, "Michael Jordan is a coach's dream and a coach's nightmare at the same time. He knows that there are ways for him to short-cut things and beat the system. So for every incredible thing he does, he does something that defies the rules of the game. Like when the double team comes at him, instead of passing the ball, he beats the double team."

To the great surprise of many, Knight, the harshest coaching taskmaster of them all, took a lenient approach with Jordan. "The first few times he did that [leaving his feet with the ball] in practice," said C. M. Newton, who assisted Knight in coaching the 1984 Olympic team, "Coach Knight would stop practice and explain to him why it was wrong. But then we noticed that he could hang in the air for so long and do so many things with the ball that he was almost always successful. So we stopped coaching him after that." Knight, who had much less patience with another freewheeling future professional star, Charles Barkley, and cut him from the Olympic squad, says simply that Jordan is the best player he has ever worked with.

To Jordan's new teammates with the Chicago Bulls, and to his new coach, Kevin Loughery, it was evident from the earliest days of training camp in the fall of 1984 that he was a very special player. "If I put him with the starters, they win," Loughery raved. "If I put him with the second team, they win. If I put him on the offensive team, it seems his team always scores. When I put him on the defensive team, they always stop the offensive team. No matter what I do with Michael, his team wins."

His teammates were no less impressed. "The first couple of weeks in training camps we'd be running

No rookie in NBA history has elicited the kind of response from the public as did Jordan. Though grateful for the rewards his celebrity has brought him, Jordan has at times found fame to be a burden: "If I want to go to a movie, I go to the late show. If I want to get my hair cut, I go to a place where the barber closes at night and then opens up again to take me. If I want to go to a restaurant, I call ahead and see if they have a booth or table in the back."

these drills and Michael would be going full speed, slam dunking forwards, backwards and every which way," Steve Johnson, a veteran forward on the team, said. "With his being here, a positive attitude spread through the team." Anticipating the opening of the season and Jordan's debut in front of the long-suffering Bulls' fans, Bernie Lincicome, a sports columnist with the *Chicago Tribune*, wrote, "One almost expected him to be launched like a new nuclear destroyer by having some patient Bulls season ticket holder crack a bottle of champagne over his head."

Though Jordan's unveiling proved somewhat anticlimactic—hampered by a rare case of nerves, he shot a poor 5 for 16 and committed five turnovers in the Bulls' home opener, which Chicago won nevertheless—it took him only a short time to demonstrate to the rest of the league what the Bulls already knew. Praise was showered upon him after virtually every performance on his first tour around the league. Said Milwaukee Bucks coach Don Nelson: "He was sensational. Down the stretch, we couldn't do anything with him. We tried double-teaming him and he just jumped right over it." From Mike Dunleavy, then a sharpshooting Milwaukee guard and later one of the league's most astute coaches: "He showed tremendous poise. Very few rookies can come into the league and dominate like this kid." At Madison Square Garden, a capacity crowd of skeptical New Yorkers exploded when Jordan punctuated an incandescent 33-point performance with a ferocious tomahawk dunk. A few days later, across the Hudson River, in Piscataway, the coach of the New Jersey Nets, Stan Albeck, could barely contain his praise: "Michael Jordan is not only a great scorer, he is a great passer. He has unbelievable hang time. He can stay up there, jump over the double team, and then have the innate ability to get the ball to the open man no matter where he is on the floor. That part of his game isn't talked about enough." To T. R. Dunn of the Denver Nuggets, who was then regarded as the NBA's best defensive guard and harried Jordan into a subpar performance, there were simply no weaknesses in the Chicago rookie's game: "He can shoot, penetrate, pass, handle the ball and whew, everyone knows he can jump."

As word of Jordan's aerial displays spread, the Bulls played before sellouts in virtually every arena in the league—except, initially, in Chicago, where many years of miserable performances by the home-town team had left the fans somewhat jaded—and were treated to exhibitions of fan and media interest usually reserved for touring rock stars. Chicago forward Orlando Woolridge likened going on the road with Jordan to touring with Michael Jackson, and sportswriters began referring to the team as "Michael and the Jordanaires," an allusion to Elvis Presley's backup vocal group of the same name. At the halfway point of the season, Jordan led his team in scoring, assists, and steals and was second in rebounding.

The ultimate imprimatur came from Larry Bird of the Boston Celtics. Then in the midst of the second

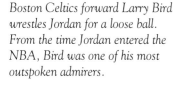

Boston Celtics forward Larry Bird wrestles Jordan for a loose ball. From the time Jordan entered the NBA, Bird was one of his most outspoken admirers.

of his three straight MVP years, "Larry Legend" was "the man"—first among the league's nobility, unchallenged as the NBA's best all-around player, and widely regarded, with Magic Johnson, as the league's savior for his role in bringing the NBA to an unprecedented height of popularity from an abyss of drug scandals, mediocre play, and negative racial stereotyping that had threatened to sink it. After watching Jordan tally 41 points, 12 rebounds, and 7 assists in a close loss at home to his Celtics, the league's defending champions, the laconic Bird, who customarily doled out praise sparingly, was positively effusive in his praise of Jordan. "I have never seen one player turn around a team like that," Bird said. "All the Bulls have become better because of him, and pretty soon this place will be packed every night, not just when the Celtics come to town. They'll pay just to watch Jordan. Got to."

To Bird, Jordan already was, simply, "the best. Never seen anyone like him. Unlike anyone I've ever seen. Phenomenal. One of a kind. He's the best. Ever." Asked if that meant even better than himself, the proud Bird replied, "Yep. At this stage in his career, he's doing more than I ever did. I couldn't do what he did as a rookie. Heck, there was one drive tonight. He had the ball up in his right hand, then he took it down, then he put it back up. I got a hand on it, fouled him, and he still scored. And all the while he's in the air. You have to play this game to know how difficult that is. You see that and figure, 'Well, what the heck can you do?'" ✧

5

AIR JORDAN

N OT ALL OF the NBA's superstars were as gracious as Bird in welcoming the high-flying newcomer to their ranks. When the fans responded to Jordan's exploits by electing him to a starting position on the Eastern Conference squad for the 1985 All-Star Game, some of Jordan's peers decided that the league's annual midseason showcase offered a prime opportunity to give him what they regarded as a badly needed lesson in humility.

Jordan's success had aroused no small amount of jealousy among his colleagues. No player had elicited such adulation from the fans so quickly, but in large part Jordan's trouble with his colleagues began before he had even set foot on an NBA floor. Though some had doubts about the level of success he would ultimately attain as a professional player, Jordan himself had none, and he entered his contract negotiations with the Bulls with the express goal of becoming, in his own words, the "best marketed" athlete in America. This ambition was shared by the agent he selected to represent him, David Falk, an aggressive Washington, D.C., sports attorney, and was achieved by obtaining national endorsement

Many observers of the NBA predicted that Jordan's high-flying, reckless style would expose him to injury, but through his rookie year the Chicago superstar showed no inclination to pace himself.

73

A Chicago public school official accepts a donation of $200,000—written as a check on the side of a pair of Air Jordans—from Jordan. Jordan has enjoyed greater success as an endorser of products than any athlete in history, but his role as a commercial pitchman has exposed him to the jealousy of colleagues and criticism for his alleged insensitivity to social issues.

deals for McDonald's, for Coca-Cola, and most important, for Nike athletic shoes.

The Nike deal was unprecedented. Jordan, an untested rookie, would be paid $500,000 dollars a year for five years to wear Nike basketball sneakers. (Only the great center for the Los Angeles Lakers, Kareem Abdul-Jabbar, who had been in the league for 18 years and would go on to score more points than anyone in NBA history, had a sneaker deal that paid him in six figures annually, and he received $100,000 each year.) In addition, a special sneaker and a line of athletic clothing, bearing Jordan's name, would be created specifically for him, and he would receive a royalty on each such item sold. Nike committed itself to spending several million dollars in promoting Jordan's sportswear and shoes.

Most people involved in the burgeoning sports-apparel industry thought Nike had made a very foolish deal. No professional athlete, let alone a rookie, had ever been paid that kind of money to wear a sneaker, and very few thought that Nike would recoup its investment, let alone reap meaningful profits. Gordie Nye, vice president of Reebok, a competing manufacturer of athletic shoes and clothing, said of Jordan, "When he came out of college, everybody knew he would be a premium player. What was not predicted was that he would be such a quantum improvement over the spokesmen of the time. No one person had ever been able to drive a business the way he drove it." According to David Falk, "Michael was considered a very flashy player, but not a dominating player, not a complete player. No one really had an idea of how good he was, partially because of the system at North Carolina, and partly because he was really a late bloomer. It was obvious that he was going to be marketable, *pretty* marketable, but we really didn't have any glimpse that he would be the most prolific team sports personality of all time." Nike's management even had some doubts about the wisdom of the arrangement and included several escape clauses in its agreement with Jordan: it could discontinue making the Jordan line if he failed, in his first three years in the league, to make the All-Star or All-League team or if Nike failed in that time to receive a specified minimum number of orders—$3 million worth—for his sneaker.

But the most significant reservation Jordan had to overcome had nothing to do with his ability, but with the color of his skin. Most American corporations at the time were simply not comfortable using black males as their pitchmen, and no black athlete, no matter how accomplished, had yet achieved a significant level of commercial success. As Falk put it, there existed "a sort of sub-rosa feeling that very few people would openly communicate, but there was a general feeling lurking beneath the surface that black team-sport athletes were not marketable, that they would not be acceptable to corporate America. Not so much by the people, not so much by the consuming populace, but by the people who were making the decisions to put them on television."

As he had done with the qualified appraisals of his on-court talent, Jordan made such reservations look silly. At Falk's suggestion, Nike called the shoe it designed for his client the Air Jordan, a name designed to capitalize on Jordan's image as the most daring of basketball's aerial acrobats. The first television commercials for the sneaker appeared in mid-October 1984, about two weeks before the start of Jordan's rookie campaign. Because the sneakers were red and black, rather than the red and white of Chicago's uniform, the Bulls and the NBA were then trying to forbid Jordan from wearing them in a game, a shortsighted mistake that Nike's marketing team was quick to exploit. The commercial consisted of a camera panning from court level up Jordan's body as he stood silently, scowling, pounding a basketball angrily into the hardwood. A voice-over solemnly informed the viewer: "On October 15, Nike created a revolutionary new basketball shoe. On October 18, the NBA threw them out of the game. Fortunately, the NBA can't keep you from wearing them. Air Jordans. For Nike."

The combination of the forbidden with Jordan's imaginative, charismatic play proved irresistible to the young consumers targeted by Nike, while his warm, open, nonthreatening public persona made him something of an All-American boy with their parents. He never made public statements about racial issues, for example; was known to eschew drugs and alcoholic drink; was publicly and properly proud of the gold medal he had won representing the United States of America; and was unfailingly cooperative with fans and the media. "The thing about Jordan is that he doesn't alienate anybody," said Gordie Nye. On Thanksgiving 1984, as Jordan was making his first soaring sweep around the league, Nike unveiled a new commercial. Over the low roar of airplane engines, viewers were treated to an aerial view of the Chicago skyline while a voice, presumably from a control tower, told an airplane captain: "Ready for takeoff." Cut to Jordan rising through the air toward the hoop, legs split, ball palmed in his right hand in front of him, left arm extended out behind him. As Jordan slammed the ball down through the hoop, a voice-over asked: "Who said man was not meant to fly?"

In its first year of production alone, Nike sold $130 million worth of Air Jordans and nearly $20

Jordan's popularity as a professional player was so great that he was single-handedly responsible for introducing an enduring on-court fashion trend: long, loose baggy shorts, worn almost to the knee, over bicycle-racing shorts.

million more of Jordan sports apparel. Had Air Jordan been its own company—and respondents to marketing polls often indicated that they believed it was—that sales figure would have made it the fifth-largest manufacturer of athletic shoes in the world. Sales climbed even higher in succeeding years, and across America Air Jordans became the single most desirable item of athletic apparel. Jordan's popularity was such that he was single-handedly responsible for beginning two other on-court fashion trends as well: looser-cut, baggy, long (almost to the knee) basketball shorts, and longer, tightly wrapped spandex bicycle-style shorts beneath them. Once Jordan began taking the court in the baggy shorts he preferred, countless younger players across the country did the same.

Jordan's instantaneous popularity did not sit well with many of the NBA's longer established stars, especially Magic Johnson and Isiah Thomas. Long before Jordan's arrival, Johnson reveled in his image as the league's preeminent black star, and his popularity had been such that, with Bird, he was generally credited with restoring the NBA's popular appeal and, indeed, raising it to new heights. His play had, in addition, done much to dispel noxious racial stereotypes about blacks as selfish, self-indulgent players more naturally talented than hardworking, more interested in flashy individual accomplishment than team play. But controversies with teammates over his salary, his contract, and his perceived role in personnel decisions had brought him into conflict with Abdul-Jabbar over who should be the highest-paid Laker and left fellow players uncertain as to whether Magic was not in fact more a member of management than one of them; and his performance in the finals of the 1984 playoffs, in which his ghastly failures of nerve and execution had, in all likelihood, cost his team the championship, had worn even more of the shine off Johnson's star.

Johnson's popularity had suffered accordingly, and whereas it had once seemed that he would be the black athlete to break through commercially, Jordan had beaten him to it. If there is one single characteristic common to all world-class athletes, it is a relentless competitiveness, extending often beyond the arena to matters of contracts, endorsements, and other marks of stature and rewards to the ego. Johnson's irritation at Jordan's accession was only aggravated by the fact that the new Chicago star had rebuffed the Laker great's suggestion that he make Dr. Charles Tucker, who was Johnson's agent, his own business representative as well. (Not long afterward, Johnson would sever his ties with Tucker, and with his new agent, Lon Rosen, his off-the-court income would skyrocket.)

Thomas's animosity toward Jordan stemmed from similar sources. The diminutive Pistons' stalwart was Johnson's best friend—indeed, their extremely close relationship had given rise to a unique pregame custom: before the tipoff of each game between Detroit and Los Angeles, they kissed, "a pregame salute," said Magic, "to our friendship and respect for the game"—and his competitive fires burned no less brightly. Like Johnson, he aspired to championships, money, and popularity, but though his prodigious talent was comparable—"Pocket Magic" he had been dubbed—his team, unlike Johnson's perennially powerful squad, was still just barely mediocre, and unlike Johnson's trademark broad grin, Thomas's angelic, boyish smile was widely held to disguise a nature that was petulant and sneaky. Jordan's arrival had hurt Thomas directly. Upon signing the Bulls' rookie to a lucrative endorsement deal for a signature line of basketballs, Wilson, a sporting-goods manufacturer, had immediately dropped Thomas from a similar deal. Mark Aguirre, all-star forward of the Dallas Mavericks and close friend of both Thomas and Johnson, was also axed by Wilson at the same time.

According to a variety of sources, Thomas and Johnson decided that the 1985 NBA All-Star Game, which was played in Indianapolis, Indiana, was a good place for Jordan to pay some dues. Aggravated anew when Jordan competed in the annual slam-dunk competition, held the day before the game, wearing gold chains and a new, specially designed Nike warm-up suit—the other competitors wore their team's uniforms, and it appeared to many as if Jordan were flaunting his Nike deal—Thomas engineered a "freeze-out" of Jordan by some of his Eastern Conference teammates, while Johnson made certain that the man Jordan was guarding, George "the Iceman" Gervin, a preternaturally gifted scorer, got the ball as often as possible. Though Thomas and Johnson have always denied participating in such a scheme, a Detroit sportswriter reported encountering the two of them, Gervin, and Tucker chortling about it at the airport after the game, and observers noted frequent occasions during the contest when Jordan was open and did not receive the ball, as well as a noticeable reluctance on the part of several of his teammates to come to his defensive aid with Gervin.

For whatever reason, Jordan hardly acquitted himself in the All-Star Game like the brightest of the NBA's new stars. He shot an abysmal two for nine from the floor, committed several turnovers, and had a rough time handling the Iceman. Apprised afterward of the alleged cabal, Jordan, who beforehand could scarcely contain his excitement about the contest—"God, I just know I'll be so happy playing in that game"—was nearly distraught. "That makes me feel very small," he said. "I want to crawl inside a hole and not come out. I'll go home and mope the rest of the day."

Jordan was learning in other ways as well that his ability and drive made him a man apart. As the season progressed, it became painfully apparent to him that none of his fellow Chicago Bulls shared his commitment to the game or to winning. A large part of the reason had been made apparent at a postgame party to which Jordan had been invited early in the season; he arrived to find many of his teammates grotesquely stoned or drunk and cocaine being circulated openly. Appalled, he made some awkward apologies and quickly excused himself. From that point on, he largely confined his off-court socializing with teammates to movie forays and marathon Ping-Pong and pool sessions in the recreation room of his newly purchased suburban Chicago town house with Rod Higgins, a similarly clean living Chicago forward.

Energized by Jordan, the Bulls had played well early in the year, but after the All-Star break they began to fade. To the team's leading scorer the previous season, Quintin Dailey, whose starting job Jordan had taken, the reason was clear: the coaching staff's preferential treatment of the team's new star. "Michael didn't ask for it, but he was their boy," Dailey told a Chicago newspaperman just before the All-Star Game, "their" in this case referring to Chicago coaches Kevin Loughery and Fred Carter. "And I was at the other end, the one who could do nothing right. Jordan's got great natural talent, but he's still learning the NBA game. But even when he'd take a messed-up shot or throw a bad pass during the preseason, Loughery and Carter would be clapping their hands and giving him encouragement and everything."

There was some truth in what Dailey said, for Loughery's approach epitomized that of all Jordan's coaches in the first part of his career in the NBA. Realizing that their undermanned and disunited team would go only as far as Jordan could take it, Loughery and his successors tended to give him almost total freedom and let his outsized talent and will carry the Bulls as far as they could.

Jordan had another explanation for Chicago's failures: "I've always said, the best talent I've ever played with was my first year with the Bulls. But I call them 'the Looney Tunes.' Physically, they were the best. Mentally, they weren't even close."

Perhaps the most talented, and certainly the most troubled, was Quintin Dailey. An unorthodox, natural-born scorer who was orphaned as a teenager when both his parents died unexpectedly within a month of one another, Dailey had the dubious distinction of then being the only NBA player single-handedly responsible for the demise of the basketball program at a major university. (His alma mater, the University of San Francisco, had ended its program after Dailey's arrest and conviction for sexual assault on a student nurse.) He had nonetheless been Chicago's first-round draft choice in 1982, and he had excelled, making the league's All-Rookie team, but the following season, having elevated his scoring average to a very fine 18 points a game and his cocaine habit to All-League status as well, he attempted suicide and had to be hospitalized for depression. In 1985, a short time after making his comments about Jordan, Dailey tested positive for cocaine in a league-mandated drug test and was suspended. His career from that point onward would be a hellish succession of failed drug tests, suspensions, stays in drug rehabilitation centers, weight problems, and unsuccessful efforts to regain his on-court form.

Other Bulls had peculiarities of their own. Orlando Woolridge, Chicago's best scorer after Jordan, would also eventually land in drug rehabili-

By January 1985, when this photograph was taken, the sight of Jordan gliding by a hapless defender for another two points had become a familiar one to NBA players, coaches, and fans. According to Chicago assistant coach John Bach, Jordan consistently displayed a "wanton disregard for his defender."

tation. Center Jawann Oldham, a prodigious leaper and shot blocker, possessed a personality so menacing and unpredictable that several teammates and at least one Chicago coach were afraid to be alone with him in the same room. Talented young playmaker Ennis Whatley struggled with drug and personal problems that would ultimately drive him from the league. Strong rebounder Sidney Green carried a reputation, deserved or not, as an uncooperative "coach killer." Center-forward Steve Johnson, an adept low-post scorer, was perenially overweight and unhappy with his contract.

Two days after the All-Star Game, Jordan repaid Thomas for his disrespect with a frighteningly dominant performance in which he soared for 49 points and 16 rebounds in a 13-point Chicago defeat of Detroit in overtime, but for the most part the second half of the season was devoid of highlights for Jordan and his supporting cast. Jordan's play continued to be exceptional, but over one stretch the team lost 12 straight road games, and Jordan appeared so fatigued that Loughery chose to rest him for the last 10 minutes of a game against the Washington Bullets that his star regarded as still close enough to win. Loughery's decision elicited some pointed barbs from Jordan—not the last time that his teammates and coaches would hear critical commentary from him.

Though the Bulls finished the regular season with 38 wins and 44 losses, their record was still good enough to earn them a spot in the playoffs, not an

For Jordan, his rookie season marked the first in a series of campaigns in which his outstanding individual accomplishments proved small consolation for his team's lack of success. Over the years, Jordan often found it very difficult to understand why his teammates could not attain his level of excellence.

exceptional feat in itself, since approximately two-thirds of NBA teams qualify for the so-called second season, but one that Chicago had nonetheless failed to accomplish in several years. His teammates were jubilant, but Jordan was not overly elated. The season had been the first in which he played on a losing team, and Chicago was quickly and easily eliminated in the first round by the Milwaukee Bucks.

There were still many reasons for satisfaction. Jordan had led his team in scoring (more than 28 points per game), rebounding (more than six per game, despite playing guard), and assists (almost six per game). To lead a team in just scoring and assists is an exceptionally rare accomplishment, but Jordan's feat had been achieved by just two players before him: the great Boston Celtics center Dave Cowens and the hallowed Larry Bird. He was the nearly unanimous winner of the league's Rookie of the Year award. He was a fan favorite, as measured in commercial endorsements and the sheer number of ticket buyers who paid their way into NBA arenas to see him play. (Chicago's average attendance per game in 1983–84, the year before Jordan's arrival, was a sickly 6,365. In Jordan's rookie year, that figure rose to nearly 12,000; by 1988, it was 17,794—a sellout. Competing franchises banked on capacity crowds every night the Bulls were in town.)

And despite the All-Star Game incident, his play had earned the admiration of his peers. Asked by a reporter whether the rookie Jordan had to win a championship before he could be considered to be in the same class as Bird or Johnson, Basketball Hall of Famer K. C. Jones, coach of the Celtics, was quick to respond. "He's there," Jones said. "How many games does he have to play to show he belongs in that class? He was there from the time the first ball was thrown up in the first Bulls' game." ✧

6

GOD IN DISGUISE

◖◗

With his broken foot in a walking cast, a disconsolate Jordan watches from the sidelines in December 1985 as his teammates drop another contest.

J ORDAN BEGAN his quest for the championship that would validate his greatness as an employee of a new Chicago Bulls organization. Real estate magnate Jerry Reinsdorf had bought the team near the close of Jordan's rookie season and replaced Rod Thorn as general manager with Jerry Krause, who in turn fired Kevin Loughery as coach in favor of Stan Albeck. Over time, Jordan would prove to be less than thrilled with all of these developments. Reinsdorf, he would feel at various points, was committed less to excellence and winning a championship than to profits. Jordan took no great exception to Albeck, but he did, despite his publicly expressed criticism, miss Loughery, whom he would later regard as his favorite of the men who coached him in the professional ranks. "I feel like I was able to relate better with him than with any coach I ever had," Jordan said once about the fiery Loughery, who with the Bulls set a single-season record for technical fouls. "He was a player's coach. He liked my game and wanted me to be a leader." For Jordan, who once said that "the truth was I didn't know how good I'd become or what I could do against the pros," the confidence that

Loughery showed in him when he was just an untried rookie endeared the coach to him forever.

But Jordan's greatest objection would be to Jerry Krause, the general manager, whom he regarded as lacking both style and substance. Krause was rotund and rumpled and had never played the game; as Jordan's frustration mounted with the passing of the years and Chicago's failure to win a championship, he began to regard himself as infinitely more qualified to make player personnel decisions than the loquacious general manager who boasted to anyone who would listen of his acuity as a talent scout. Jordan dubbed Krause, who has never been accused of being well dressed, "Crumbs" because, he said, the short and stout general manager always had doughnut crumbs on his lapels, and he often led his teammates in a chorus of mooing when Krause entered the locker room. Krause returned Jordan's animosity; he regarded his best player as meddlesome and egotistical and at times during Chicago's quest for the ring

Jordan's acrobatic style made him a prime candidate for a foot injury. Because of the constant impact on them resulting from running and jumping, injuries to the feet were very common among NBA players in the 1970s and early 1980s. Today, improved footwear has greatly reduced the problem.

complained that if the Bulls had only had the good fortune to draft Hakeem Olajuwon instead, he—Krause—would have "won two championships already."

The two men's discontent with one another stemmed from a mutual frustration born of a shared commitment to winning; it manifested itself over the years in major quarrels over several specific issues. The first, and in many ways the most serious, took place in 1985–86, Jordan's second year in the NBA.

To Jordan's dismay—he has, throughout his career, constantly hectored Chicago management to upgrade the quality of the on-court talent—the turnover in the organization's personnel did not extend to the players. The Bulls began the season with essentially the same roster as the previous year, and Jordan's forebodings seemed to be justified in the preseason when the team lost all eight of its exhibition contests. Then, just before the start of the regular season, a seemingly rejuvenated Quintin Dailey announced that he needed a short sabbatical for another stay in a drug rehabilitation center. To bolster the suddenly depleted Chicago backcourt, Krause went out and acquired San Antonio's George Gervin. "Just say that I am unhappy about it" was all the seething Jordan would say for public consumption about the trade. Gervin had been, of course, a key participant in Jordan's All-Star Game comeuppance. More important, the Iceman's once exquisite game had declined precipitously as a result of encroaching age and an intensifying fondness for cocaine. To make matters worse, the Bulls cut Rod Higgins, Jordan's only friend on the team, just before the season started.

The Bulls managed to win their season opener and their second contest, a matchup with the Pistons that nearly degenerated into a riot after Bill Laimbeer essentially hauled Jordan from midair on a drive and hurled him to the floor. Shortly before halftime in

Bulls owner Jerry Reinsdorf (left) and general manager Jerry Krause flank Jordan at a February 15, 1986, press conference called to discuss the condition of his injured left foot. Until the injury, Jordan had never missed a game in high school, college, or professional ball.

game three, on October 29, 1985, Jordan broke the navicular tarsal bone in his left foot while running upcourt. It was initially estimated that the small fracture—so small that it required a CAT scan rather than an X ray to detect—in the tiny bone would keep him out of action for just three to six weeks, but it would be four-and-a-half months and 63 games before Jordan returned.

The navicular tarsal bone is one of the smallest in the body; as a result, it receives a limited blood flow, and accurate predictions about the rate and extent of its recovery once injured are notoriously difficult to make. Though Jordan reacted poorly to the diagnosis of the first major injury he had suffered in his athletic career—he intended, he said, to go home and cry—he was diligent in following the rehabilitation program prescribed by his doctors. The bone simply would not respond.

Meanwhile, without him, the Bulls, predictably, fell apart and began to free-fall toward the bottom of the league standings. Immensely frustrated, Jordan decamped to Wilmington, where he steadfastly refused Krause's entreaties to rejoin the team as a spectator. Negative stories in the Chicago newspapers proliferated after a photograph was taken of Jordan sitting on the University of North Carolina bench next to Dean Smith. Krause pled some more; Jordan said that he could not stand to sit and watch the way his teammates were playing. Right before the February All-Star Game break, Quintin Dailey, who had been spirited out of rehab when Jordan got injured, tested positive again for cocaine and was suspended. Jordan was realistic but unsympathetic, saying that Dailey had let his team down when it needed him and that he could not be relied on in the future. Shortly afterward, an admittedly depressed Jordan returned to Chicago for a team meeting and called some of his teammates, to their face, quitters. The predictable outcry left him essentially unfazed. "I'm not trying to create a controversy," he said, "but I believe a hurt dog will holler. I didn't say the whole team wasn't trying, just certain guys."

Soon, Jordan's doubts about the competitive instincts of others would extend to the Chicago front office and ownership. As the season approached its end and the Bulls continued their pitiful play, it was suggested that it might be in everybody's best interest if Jordan did not return that year. At best, even with a returned and healthy Jordan, the Bulls might sneak into the playoffs, where they would likely be eliminated in the first round. But if Jordan were not to return, he would have more time to rest his foot, and the Bulls would in all likelihood miss the playoffs—an outcome desirable in some ways because it would give the organization the chance to compete in the lottery for the first selection in that year's college draft.

Only nonplayoff teams participated in the lottery, where, even if Chicago did not get the top pick, it would nevertheless have the opportunity to draft from the cream of the college crop. Jordan was good enough, almost, to single-handedly drag the Bulls into the playoffs every year, but unless management

March 10, 1986: Jordan practices with the Bulls for the first time since fracturing his foot in late October of the previous year. That night, a CAT scan revealed a tiny new fracture in his left foot, which Jordan determined to ignore.

improved his supporting cast, even his brilliance would not be sufficient to carry the team past the opening round. Though a tribute to its team's ineptitude, the opportunity thus presented to Chicago management—to enter the lottery—therefore represented what would probably be a rare chance to improve the team dramatically.

Meanwhile, unbeknownst to Chicago management and his doctors, Jordan, convinced that his foot had healed no matter what CAT scans told his physicians, had begun to take part in pick-up games—"when I finally dunked it felt wonderful"—in Woollen Gym in Chapel Hill. Although Jordan desperately wanted management to improve the team, to do so by not putting the best team on the floor was an affront to his athletic ethos. When he began to suspect that that was exactly what Krause and Reinsdorf wanted to do, his attitude grew even more antagonistic. He returned to Chicago on March 10, 1986, to practice with the team, but that night yet another CAT scan revealed another small crack in the bone, and doctors advised that he not play until the following season to reduce the risk of even greater injury.

Krause and Reinsdorf agreed, but Jordan insisted that he knew better than the doctors. Against their better judgment, the owner and general manager agreed to allow him to play, but within severe restrictions—Jordan would be allowed to play no more than seven minutes per half.

The compromise, which led to some bizarre scenarios, only compounded Jordan's frustration. In his first game back, on March 15 against the Milwaukee Bucks, he played his alloted total of 14 minutes, only to be told by Coach Albeck, who was under intense pressure from Krause and Reinsdorf, that he could not play at all when the game went into overtime. Chicago lost. Two days later, Jordan, in a seven-minute fourth-quarter stint, rallied his teammates from behind to an eight-point lead over the Atlanta Hawks. But with just under two minutes to go, his time was up, and he was pulled off the floor. Chicago lost as, with Jordan fuming on the bench, his head draped in a towel, the Hawks scored the game's last 18 points. Irate, Jordan insisted that the restrictions be lifted and told a reporter that he thought he would have to "fight Krause." Two days later, the same scenario replayed itself as Jordan led his teammates to a lead late in the fourth quarter, which they then blew when he was ordered to the bench.

By April, Jordan's alloted minutes were up to 14 a half, but he was still dissatisfied, now absolutely convinced that Krause, who argued that he was simply trying to protect the future of the franchise's most important asset, wanted Chicago to lose games and miss out on the playoffs. "Losing games on purpose reflects what kind of person you are," Jordan said. "No one should ever try to lose to get something better. You always try to make the best with what you have. If they really wanted to make the playoffs, I'd be in there whenever we had a chance to win a game." He then, on April 2, mistakenly or knowingly, insisted that his doctor had told him that his foot had improved enough to play an entire game, and that if Krause said anything different, he was a liar. Krause said what in fact the doctor had told him: No improvement in Jordan's foot could be detected.

The situation reached its logical absurdity the next night. With 30 seconds to go and Chicago up by a point, Jordan's time ran out and Albeck pulled him from the game. Krause, who was in attendance, believed the coach had allied himself with Jordan and removed him from the game to make a mockery of management; the incident was generally believed to be responsible for Albeck's being fired at the conclusion of the season.

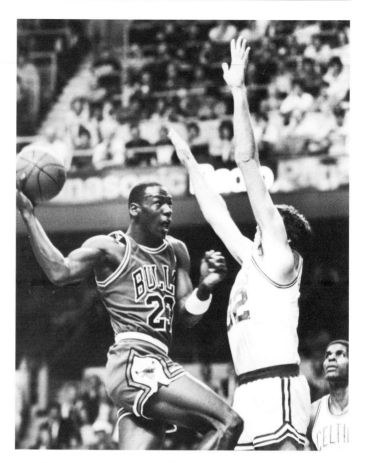

Having missed 63 games of the regular season, it was an extremely energetic and well-rested Jordan who took the floor against the Boston Celtics in the first round of the 1986 playoffs. As the Celtics' Robert Parish looks on, his teammate Kevin McHale attempts to stop Jordan's foray to the hoop.

On April 11, with Chicago trailing at home by eight points at halftime against the Washington Bullets but able, with a win, to clinch a playoff spot, Reinsdorf announced to the capacity crowd in attendance that there would be no limits on Jordan's playing time in the second half. The Bulls came back to win the game and sneak into the playoffs, despite their abysmal record. Afterward, Jordan said of Reinsdorf, "He took the risk and gave me the chance to play. So he is a kind man. He does have a heart." He would not be so forgiving of Krause.

As management had feared, the Bulls' late-season surge—they won four of their last six games—allowed them to serve as sacrificial lambs in the playoffs. As the Eastern Conference playoff team with the worst regular-season record, Chicago had earned the dubious right, in the first round, of playing the team with the best—the Boston Celtics, who were on their way to their third championship of the decade. Prognosticators rightly gave the Bulls little chance, but no one could have predicted the magnitude of Jordan's performance, which remains one of the most magnificent in basketball history.

There are ways in which the form and substance of an individual's style on the basketball court—his game, in short—transcend the significance of any particular contest in which he is playing, the outcome of which is, after all, perhaps in the larger scheme of things not so very important. A great player's game is as distinctive a means of self-expression as the tone that emerges when a trumpet player lifts his horn to his lips or a pianist sits down to his instrument; applying a physical art that at its best emulates in creativity and grace that of the dance, he may elevate the limited, hackneyed form of a single basketball game into something special, just as the jazz musician of genius, improvising on traditional elements of melody, harmony, and rhythm, makes something new and wonderful of some tired old standard or 12-bar blues.

"Basketball is like jazz in terms of improvisation," the great trumpeter Wynton Marsalis has observed. "When you are improvising in music, the obstacles are the chord changes. . . . In basketball, the obstacles are the defenders, and with the most skillful players, you can see them working their way through the obstacles to a successful resolution." The two pursuits are similar in another way as well: professional basketball and jazz are also two of the very few areas of American culture that have traditionally been dominated by blacks. "Basketball is just a game, but a man with a basketball can be so much more," the great forward Julius Erving, Jordan's forerunner in skyward creativity, once said.

Weakened by the flu, Jordan scored 49 points against the Celtics in the playoff opener, turning future Hall of Famer Dennis Johnson, one of the league's most accomplished defenders, every which way but loose. "He's by far the best guard in the league," said the shell-shocked Johnson, who had been treated to an up-close view of myriad moves from Jordan's seemingly inexhaustible repertoire. Boston coach K. C. Jones said Jordan was so dominant that when he looked down his bench for substitutes, his reserves, who usually edged eagerly forward at such moments, hoping to catch his eye, all looked the other way for fear they would be asked to go in and guard Jordan.

Thoroughly warmed up, Jordan scored an incomprehensible 63 points against the Celtics in Game 2, going over and around a host of bewildered Boston defenders. In the game's most memorable sequence,

Jordan's record-shattering performance in Game 2 of his team's 1986 playoff series with the Celtics—his 63 points constituted a single-game playoff record—was all the more remarkable in that he was being guarded primarily by Dennis Johnson (rear), one of the league's most tenacious defenders.

he went mano-a-mano with Bird when the Celtic forward jumped out on a switch to guard him deep in the right corner. Juking in several different directions while dribbing the ball rapidly back and forth between his legs, Jordan created an illusion of motion that sent Bird scurrying backward, then embarked on a tortuous foray along the baseline that took him around Johnson, who had rushed to his overmatched captain's aid. Met then by Kevin McHale, the long-armed Celtic forward who was one of the league's premier shot blockers, Jordan took to the air, elevating above and beyond the reach of him and the late-arriving Boston center, Robert Parish, to emerge on the far side of the basket, where he flipped the ball off glass and through the hoop.

"I think he's God disguised as Michael Jordan," an appreciative Bird said after the game, his mood no doubt lightened by the fact that his team had withstood the onslaught to triumph in double overtime. "No question he had control of the game. He had to have one of the greatest feelings you can ever have. And, as hard it might be to believe, it's actually fun playing against a guy like that." Bird, who placed toughness and single-mindedness above all other virtues, was as impressed by Jordan's just stepping on the court as he was by his performance there: "One thing I really like about him is that he said he was ready to play, even though management said no. He fought to come back. There was no question management wanted to get into the draft lottery. I think that takes a lot of guts. It shows what kind of person he is. He is the most awesome player in the NBA."

"I was watching, and all I could see was this giant Jordan and everyone else was sort of in the background," K. C. Jones added. "I feel I showed the Bulls management that I am a very competent young man and that I can make my own decisions," said the unforgiving Jordan. ❦

7

JORDAN RULES

*J*ORDAN TIRED badly in the third game against Boston, allowing the Celtics to hold him to only 19 points, 10 assists, and 9 rebounds and complete their sweep of the Bulls, but after a summer of rest he was ready to resume his assault on the record books. Only two players in NBA history—Wilt Chamberlain and the elegant Elgin Baylor, another Jordan forerunner in hang time and grace—have ever scored as prolifically as did Jordan in the 1986–87 season, and neither of those players was a guard.

For Jordan, the season was a cavalcade of personal highlights. He claimed his first scoring championship, with an ungodly average of 37.1 points per game. He scored 50 points or more in a game nine separate times; at one stretch he accomplished the feat three games in succession. He scored 61 points in a game twice. Over one stretch, he scored 40 points or more in a game in nine consecutive contests. In the season opener, he served notice of things to come by scoring 50 points against the New York Knicks; three weeks later, against the same opponent, he scored his team's final 18 points, including the game-winning jump shot with eight seconds left to play. Later in the season, he set an NBA record by scoring

"I think one outstanding aspect is he's always playing the game low. . . . His ability to accelerate and stop are two things that are better than anybody. Anybody I've seen, anyway. He's always got the gun cocked." Thus Hall of Fame coach Pete Newell described the "mechanics" of Jordan's game.

23 consecutive points against the Atlanta Hawks. When Philadelphia's Charles Barkley threatened to "break him up in little pieces" to keep his scoring in check, Jordan notched 47. In his last matchup with the revered Julius Erving, who had once said that watching Jordan play was "like looking in a mirror," Jordan scored 56, on a night that Chicago as a team managed just 93. In addition to his prodigious offensive display, Jordan became the first player in NBA history to record more than 100 blocked shots and 200 steals in the same season.

The by-now-usual encomiums followed in his wake: Boston's Bill Walton, after Jordan tossed in a casual 48 against his team, said, "You get numbed to the spectacular in this league, and I practice with Larry Bird every day, but Jordan, he is unbelievable." According to Jack Ramsay, the scholarly coach of the Indiana Pacers, Jordan was "the best offensive player I've seen. Just creatively, with the ball, he's probably the best ever. When he gets to the basket he's tough, because he's in the air. It's tough to defend a player in the air. . . . Larry Bird and Magic Johnson require their special games, but Jordan is in a class by himself in that respect."

The highest vote getter in the balloting for the All-Star Game, Jordan won the mid-season slam-dunk contest with his patented "kiss-the-rim" jam. Chicago played before 316,000 more fans than the previous season, all of them seemingly frantic for an up-close and in-person glimpse of the phenomenon. A set of new commercials for Nike, directed by acclaimed filmmaker Spike Lee, lifted his popularity even more and made him a seemingly ubiquitous television presence, and he was the subject of laudatory profiles by Tom Brokaw on "NBC Nightly News" and Diane Sawyer on "60 Minutes," as well as numerous articles in the print media. (Sawyer's piece was so adulatory that Jordan's agent referred to it joyfully as "our 10-minute commercial.") He became, clearly, the most emulated and admired athlete in America. ("He's emulated by every kid in the community," James Naughton quotes a Chicago schoolteacher as saying in *Taking to the Air*. "They wear Jordan clothes. They wear number 23. They've got his picture everywhere. He could marry any girl in any high school. I know girls whose kids are put into Jordan toddler clothes as soon as they're born.") Accommodating with the fans and the media, famously clean living, he was cited by an increasing number of authorities as an important role model for black youth, admired both for his artistry on the hardwood and business success off it. "He comes out of an area where blacks traditionally excel," said sociologist Shelby Steele, "and because he is probably the best basketball player alive, he has legendary status among blacks, who prize that game more than any other. I think they are proud of the way he conducts himself in the mainstream of American society." To make matters complete, Jordan met Juanita Vanoy, a bank officer who would become, in short succession, his most trusted confidante, mother of his first son, his wife, mother to another son and daughter, and manager of some of his business affairs.

But all Jordan's brilliance was not enough to lift Chicago above mediocrity. Though Krause had rid the team of most of those to whose game and character Jordan objected—Woolridge, Dailey, Green, Gervin, and Oldham—the rebuilding phase had not yet begun, and except for second-year man Charles Oakley, Jordan was saddled with an abject supporting cast. Chicago could manage only 40 wins before again being swept by Boston in the first round of the playoffs.

To some observers, there was something disconcerting about Jordan's dominance and the degree of emotion and effort he brought to the court. Driven by necessity, ego, or the demands of his own creative demons, he was simply trying to do too much. A sportswriter observed about a late-season contest that Jordan looked "too intense for his own good." Phil Jackson, who joined the Bulls in 1987 as an assistant coach, was both awed (at what Jordan accomplished) and appalled (at the responsibilities he took upon himself) by Jordan's game and wondered how long Jordan could sustain such a superhuman expenditure of energy. He disdainfully characterized Chicago's strategy as "Throw him the ball and then clear out and he's going to go one-on-five and everyone's going to stand there and watch and everyone's going to come running at him and maybe he makes some outstanding move and pops through or crashes to the floor and burns." Even the usually complimentary Larry Bird complained that it had become "boring" to see Jordan, who took one-third of Chicago's shots, shoot so much. For John Bach, another Chicago coach, Jordan's extraordinary skills posed a unique dilemma. "He borders on being too good," Bach said, "and by that I mean he's causing a lot of things that have always been taught in basketball, particularly relating to the team concept, to be reevaluated. I'm questioning these things myself, and I've been coaching 40 years." For example, how was one to convince Jordan that he needed to rely more on his teammates, when his dedication and talent were so clearly superior to theirs? How was Jordan to be convinced that he ought to look for the open man when there was not a defender in the league who could stop him?

The responsibility for resolving this dilemma fell on the skinny shoulders of Doug Collins, the former high-scoring guard for the Philadelphia 76ers whom Krause had installed, over Reinsdorf's objections, as Chicago's coach for the 1986–87 season. High strung, frenetic, fanatically intense, Collins admired Jordan's dedication and, with little alternative, in his first

The center of attention, as always on the basketball court, Jordan floats for two of his record 40 points in the 1988 All-Star Game, which was held in Chicago. Jordan is the NBA's all-time per-game scorer in the regular season, the playoffs, and the All-Star Game.

season simply gave him free rein to do essentially as he liked, an arrangement that made for harmonious relations between the two men.

But for coach and superstar the pressure of creating a championship team led to mounting frustration. Clearly rankled by the persistent, negative comparisons with Bird and Johnson, Jordan gave an interview before the opening of the 1987–88 season in which he disparaged the talents of his own teammates by pointing out that the Boston and Los Angeles greats were surrounded by All-Stars; anybody who did not think that it was easier for Johnson and Bird to make their teammates better (the ultimate criteria for the so-called team player, which Jordan was accused of not being), he said, was a "damn fool." Early on in the season, he announced after a game that his goal "was to show that I can play defense and that I don't shoot as much as Larry Bird would say."

Krause felt his wrath as well. The general manager was extremely pleased with his draft-day acquisitions, chiefly Brad Sellers, Scottie Pippen, and Horace Grant, but Jordan was much less so. Always loyal to players from his home state, he had wanted Krause to pick Duke guard Johnny Dawkins instead of Sellers, and it took him only a few practice sessions to conclude that Krause's selection was a hopeless stiff, a soft, thin 7-footer whose nice outside touch was more than negated by his unwillingness to mix it up under the boards and his inability to guard players his own size. Jordan was not shy about ex-pressing such opinions, in caustic fashion, to Sellers himself in practice, to such an extent that several teammates believed the newcomer was so traumatized that whatever virtues his game did possess were never able to flourish.

He was often equally and as vocally displeased with Grant and Pippen, who, though obviously more talented than Sellers, were, in Jordan's mind, insuf-ficiently serious about basketball. (The new players

Amid a trio of Bulls (from left Scottie Pippen, Horace Grant, and a shouting Jordan), Joe Dumars of the Pistons puts in an offensive rebound in the 1990 playoffs. For Jordan and his teammates, their inability to beat Detroit was galling. "I'd hate to say we get obsessed about it," Chicago guard John Paxson said, "but you don't like to get beat that way too often, so we do think about it."

got an early glimpse of Jordan's renowned competitiveness when he stormed out of a preseason scrimmage after accusing Collins of intentionally misstating the score.) For several seasons, until Grant at last came into his own, Jordan would lobby Krause to make a trade to secure the highly regarded, more experienced, and exceedingly available Buck Williams as Grant's replacement at power forward. Too impatient to wait willingly for Krause's youngsters to develop, Jordan constantly badgered the general manager to obtain veteran talent. (A later arriving Chicago rookie, B. J. Armstrong, was so unnerved by Jordan's criticisms that he took to reading biographies of geniuses, in various pursuits, in the hope of gaining some insight into Jordan's demanding personality.)

The changes made Chicago a much better team, but not quickly enough for Jordan. The Bulls won 50 games in 1987–88 and 47 in 1988–89 and advanced farther each year in the playoffs, defeating Cleveland in the opening round in 1988 and Cleveland (on the strength of Jordan's famous series-winning shot) and New York in the first two rounds in 1989. Jordan himself, in the eyes of many, was also a noticeably better player, less spectacular perhaps, but steadier, more well rounded, less insistent on attempting the impossible when the merely implausible would do. He still led the league in scoring both years—and scored an NBA record 40 points in the 1988 All-Star Game, played in Chicago—but the subtle transformation of his game was recognized following the 1987–88 season, when he was voted the first of his three (to this date) Most Valuable Player awards as well as official recognition, for the first time as well, as the league's best defensive player.

Yet he was no more satisfied, particularly as Chicago's ultimate elimination in the playoffs each season came at the hands of the dreaded Detroit Pistons. The hatred between the two teams was by now well established. Chicago and Detroit had engaged in spectacular brawls in regular season games in 1987 and 1988, and the 1988 playoffs featured the first instance of Jordan's throwing a punch—at Bill Laimbeer—at another player on the court. But for all the intensity of their dislike of the Pistons, the Bulls were unable to solve Detroit's roughhouse style.

Jordan blamed, among others, Krause. In addition to his other personnel miscalculations, before the 1988–89 season the general manager had made the serious mistake, in the estimation of his best player, of trading Charles Oakley to the New York Knicks for center Bill Cartwright. Oakley was, at the time, the league's best rebounder, Jordan's only close friend on the team, and one of the strongest, sturdiest, and most physical players in the league. For Chicago, which was most definitely not a physical team, he played the role of enforcer, meaning that he stood up for his teammates, especially Jordan, when other teams, most notably the Pistons, attempted to brutalize the Bulls. Without Oakley, Jordan felt even more exposed to Detroit's bruising tactics, and the Pistons felt even more free to try to intimidate the Bulls. The results, he believed, had been demonstrated in Game 7 of the playoff series against Detroit in 1989, when Pippen had been sent to the bench in the game's first minute with a concussion as the result of a Laimbeer elbow.

Cartwright, accordingly, received a frosty welcome from Jordan. Though ungainly, the veteran center was willing and effective. He had, however, like many big men, "bad hands," and his habit of dropping Jordan's brilliantly conceived passes drove his better coordinated teammate to distraction. According to Sam Smith, Jordan forbid his teammates to pass Cartwright the ball in the last five minutes of a close contest.

Krause blamed Collins. The coach's competitive fires burned as brightly, if possible, as Jordan's, and he was even more relentless in his criticisms of the young players, most of whom were soon at odds with him. As the frustration of not copping a championship mounted, Collins grew even more frenetic and intense, and the players began increasingly to tune him out. Like Jordan, he hectored Krause to add some more veterans to the Chicago roster, and he begged Reinsdorf to fire the general manager. To his players, he seemed by the end of the 1989 season to have come unstrung; he had become paranoid and unpredictable, banning one of his assistant coaches from practices and accusing another of plotting to take his job. Under stress, his face broke out in a hideous rash, and he developed the embarrassing habit of dissolving into tears when frustrated or angry. "You may think you've got problems with your coaches," Jordan said once to an amazed gathering of fellow All-Stars who were swapping war stories, "but, well, mine cries every day."

For the 1989–90 season, Krause replaced Collins with Phil Jackson, a selection that was generally regarded as risky. Jackson had no head-coaching experience in the NBA. Worse, he was regarded by many management types as, at best, quirky, odd, eccentric, or a crank. A resident of the counterculture haven of Woodstock, New York, Jackson was the son of a Pentecostal minister who had raised him in Montana without benefit of television or other modern appliances. In his playing days as a bearded, bushy-haired, long-armed, gawky, defensive specialist for the New York Knicks, Jackson had been a self-styled hippie, a vegetarian and antiwar activist, a student of various Eastern religions, and the only NBA player in memory to speak openly—and fondly—of his experiments with LSD.

Coach Phil Jackson had to attempt to convince Jordan to play within a system that required him to rely more heavily on his teammates than previously. An unorthodox motivator, Jackson greatly admired Jordan's competitive instinct: "Michael is a little bit of a shark. He's competitive to the extent that he'd like to beat you for your last cent and send you home without your clothes, too."

But as a head coach, Jackson demonstrated a rare capacity for patience and the ability to treat each player as an individual, qualities that proved a tonic for the young Bulls whom Collins had browbeaten. The players responded as well to his seeming lack of ego—unlike Collins, he seemed content to credit the players when Chicago won and reluctant to criticize them, at least publicly, when the team lost—and to his unorthodox motivational techniques. Jackson would splice scenes from *The Wizard of Oz* and shots of Sioux warrior purification ceremonies into Chicago game films, and he adopted the practice of personally selecting and buying a book for each Chicago player to read on road trips. Initially nonplussed, the Bulls soon learned to interpret the messages Jackson was sending them—for example, in the case of the *Wizard of Oz* segments, that their recent play lacked heart, courage, and brains.

There was one aspect of Jackson's program that Jordan resisted—the new coach's determination to install an offensive system that would get his teammates more involved in the Chicago offense. Jackson wanted his superstar to curtail his offensive output somewhat in order to give his teammates more opportunity to score. To do so, he wished Chicago to play a somewhat more patterned style of play on their own end of the floor. Previously, the only system to Chicago's offense was what Jordan's creative impulses dictated and allowed. Jackson believed that by getting all of the Bulls involved in the offense early in the game, and by getting them accustomed to taking shots from specific spots on the floor in specific situations, they would become more confident about stepping up at those crucial moments, when as even Jordan acknowledged—as against the Pistons—such defensive strategies as the Jordan Rules made it necessary for them to do so.

Jordan could accept the theory, but he was skeptical about its execution. He was confident enough in his own ability and basketball intelligence to believe that he could quickly master Jackson's system—the so-called triangle offense, which relied on movement without the ball, immediate recognition of defensive tactics, and a minimum of one-on-one play, was in actuality the brainchild of Chicago assistant coach Tex Winter—but he was less optimistic about how his teammates would adapt. "I know I can recognize what to do," he told Jackson, "but I'm not sure they can." Your teammates may not be as talented as you would like, Jackson replied, but we have to play with the talent we have. "If we run a system, everyone is going to have an opportunity to perform. They can't do the spectacular one-on-one things that you can do, but they can have some level of success and perform on some level, even in crucial situations."

Under Jackson, Chicago enjoyed its most successful regular season ever in 1989-90, with 55 wins, but their galling third straight defeat by the Pistons in the playoffs did nothing to lesson Jordan's ongoing skepticism about the triangle offense. Jordan's postseason proclamation that "we have to make some changes" referred less to his own style of play than to his continued demands that Krause upgrade the roster, principally by importing veteran sharpshooter Walter Davis, a former Tar Heel. But to Jordan's dismay, Krause decided essentially to stand pat.

It was an older, wiser, and in some ways a sadder Michael Jordan who took the court for the Chicago Bulls at the start of the 1990–91 season. Though polls showed him to be, along with comedian Bill Cosby, America's favorite television personality, and his off-court income had soared to somewhere close to $20 million per year, his public image was increas-

Chicago truly jelled as a team when Scottie Pippen (right) began to fulfill his vast potential. A six-foot-eight-inch forward, Pippen possessed the speed, quickness, and ball handling and shooting abilities of a much smaller player.

Jordan intercepts Detroit's Dennis Rodman on the way to the hoop. For all the attention that is given to scoring, no team wins the NBA championship without playing exceptional defense, and Chicago only rose to the top when it perfected a relentless, attacking defensive scheme that maximized the athletic skills of Jordan and Pippen.

ingly a subject of criticism. Some members of the black community charged that Jordan, fearful of tarnishing his carefully crafted public image, had failed to use his prominence in a socially constructive fashion; for instance, by speaking out against racism or in favor of social programs that helped the black community. He was criticized for failing to endorse publicly the black Democratic candidate, Harvey Gantt, in his 1990 race for the U.S. senator's seat from North Carolina held by right-winger Jesse Helms. When, in a series of highly publicized cases, a number of inner-city youths were killed in attempted robberies—the thieves' object was allegedly the victims' Air Jordans—Jordan's role as a pitchman for high-priced athletic goods came under attack. Air Jordans, which cost more than $100, were intentionally being marketed as a status symbol, critics charged, to that segment of the population—poor black youths—who could least afford them yet were most vulnerable to such an appeal.

Still without a championship, less than optimistic about Chicago's chances, Jordan suspected that his best basketball was already behind him. He conceded as training camp began that "people may have seen the best of me." Some of the joyfulness that had always characterized his game seemed to be missing; he played now less with abandon than with grim concentration. Once, he said, he had "more or less relaxed and enjoyed" the season, "this kids'-game time," but now basketball was "like a business." Each year, as more of his hair fell out due to stress, he had worn what remained increasingly close cropped; now he finally relented and shaved his head bald. He seldom dreamed about the game anymore—glorious dreams, where in his perception the game so slowed for him that each instant seemed an eternity in which he apprehended an infinite, precise, beautiful order in the constantly swirling shift of bodies, moving among them as absolute master, floating in that place and state of heightened awareness and ability ball-players call "the zone." Instead, his sleep was disturbed by nightmares in which some scandal or misbehavior on his part stripped him of all that he had earned.

A pessimistic Jordan agreed to play within Jackson's system, but he cautioned that "if things start going wrong, I'm going to start shooting." His feud with Krause continued unabated. When the general manager refused to pursue Davis, Jordan lashed out at him, stating that Chicago did not have the talent to win the championship and that he, Jordan, "had a good sense of players I play against . . . better than general managers who never played the game of basketball." Meanwhile, several Bulls, including all of the starters, were unhappy with their contracts, but Krause exacerbated their unhappiness by refusing to renegotiate, then pitching a multi-million-dollar offer to Toni Kukoc, a Yugoslavian player with no NBA experience. He then compounded his mistake by asking Jordan to call Kukoc and persuade him to sign with Chicago. "I don't speak no Yugoslavian," the noncompliant star told Krause.

But in the meantime, a funny thing began to happen. Chicago began to win—consistently and convincingly. Jordan was playing a slightly diminished, though still dominant, role in the Chicago offense, but there were factors other than the triangle offense that were chiefly responsible for the Bulls' rise.

The Chicago starting five had been together for three years, and the players had begun to grow into roles that complemented one another's. Pippen was starting to play to the full extent of his considerable potential, which made him, arguably, the second-best player in the league, behind only his celebrated teammate. Grant had accepted his role in the Chi-

Jordan (center) and Grant (left) separate Pippen from New York Knicks forwards Xavier McDaniel and Anthony Mason in the 1992 playoffs. Replicating the bullying tactics of the Pistons, the Knicks provided the Bulls with the sternest challenge of their championship seasons, but Jordan virtually willed his teammates to victory.

cago offense, in which he got few shots, and began to concentrate on defense and rebounding.

After trying a succession of players at point guard, the Bulls had finally settled on John Paxson, who proved uniquely suited to playing opposite Jordan. On most teams, the point guard controls the ball and makes most of the decisions on offense, but with the Bulls, those responsibilities were reserved for Jordan and, to a lesser extent, Pippen, who was almost as creative a player. The result had been a succession of confused Chicago point guards, traumatized by Jordan's predilection for waving them off the ball whenever he felt the necessity. But Paxson, though steady and reliable, was not a creator; his chief virtue as a player was his ability to nail open jump shots. When Jordan or Pippen wanted the ball, Paxson was more than content to let them handle it and "spot up" to a place on the floor where he would be in a position, should his defender leave to help out with his more offensive minded teammates, to receive a pass and convert a jump shot.

Cartwright, too, had begun to earn Jordan's respect. Jackson had suggested to Jordan a method whereby the center was sure to catch his passes— "throw it right at his face; he'll catch it," the coach advised—and Jordan had begun to appreciate the way, on defense, the shrewd Cartwright was able to throw opposing centers off their game.

It was defense, in fact, that made the real difference for Chicago. Previous coaches had taken Jordan's superb defense for granted, while fretting about harnessing his offensive skills, but Jackson recognized that Jordan's defense could be as dangerous a weapon as any in his arsenal. With Jordan, Pippen, and Grant, Chicago possessed three players with the skills and willingness to guard players of virtually any size the entire length of the floor. All were phenomenally quick, with long arms, great

Jordan struggles to escape the grasp of Portland's Clyde Drexler in the sixth and last game of the 1992 playoff finals. Holding Jordan was the only way Drexler found to slow his Chicago counterpart in the series, which ended with Chicago claiming its second straight championship.

leaping ability, rare gifts of anticipation, and the speed to double-team and press in the backcourt and still get back to pick up their assigned men. Bach called the three the "Dobermans," and Jackson unleashed them. Chicago began to devastate opponents with a series of traps and presses that led to myriad turnovers, fast breaks, and easy baskets that led to even easier wins.

As the team began to jell, Jordan began to exhibit an increased confidence in his teammates, which their ever-improving play consistently reinforced. He grew closer to Pippen, whose game blossomed, giving Chicago a two-pronged attack that no team in the league could match. The Bulls won 61 regular-season games and swept through the first two rounds of the playoff with just one loss, setting the stage for yet another showdown in the conference finals with the Pistons.

The result could not have been sweeter for Jordan, his teammates, and their fans, although it was almost anticlimactic in its easiness. With Jordan and Pippen playing superbly and taunting the Pistons at every opportunity, and the bench making timely contributions, the Bulls won in four straight games, none of them truly close. "They stole our playbook," said John Salley. "Talking junk, talking garbage, their intensity on defense, making sure there is only one shot, keeping people out of the middle, making us beat them with our jump shot. That's what we usually do." The turnaround was startling and was more than the Pistons could bear. With a few seconds left on the clock in the final game and Chicago hopelessly ahead, Isiah Thomas led the Pistons starters off the floor and to the locker room so that they would not have to congratulate the winners.

As Bach had predicted, once in the finals, Jordan would not let his team lose. Chicago's opponent was the Los Angeles Lakers, led by Magic Johnson, but even the winningest basketball player of his generation found himself hopelessly overmatched. Pippen neutralized him on defense, Jordan was routinely brilliant on both ends of the floor, and after dropping the first game at the buzzer, Chicago won four straight. "This is like a nightmare," Johnson said afterward. "I never dreamed that this would happen. I never even thought about us being dominated like this." In the jubilant Chicago locker room, Jordan clutched the gold championship trophy as if he would never let go and broke down in huge sobs.

If there had been any remaining doubt about Jordan's preeminence, it was clear to all who watched that there had been a changing of the guard. At least at this stage of their careers, with comparable supporting casts around them, Jordan was the superior player to Johnson in all phases of the game—in the championship round, he even compiled more assists than the greatest passer of the era. With Bird fading into retirement because of a back injury, there was now little doubt about who was the best basketball player in the world.

Once on top, Jordan showed no signs of being willing to relinquish his perch. By 1992, his annual off-court income, spurred by new endorsements for Hanes underwear and Gatorade and a new contract with Nike, had soared to above $30 million. That spring, having charged through the regular season with an absolutely superb 67 wins, the Bulls romped through the playoffs to their second straight championship. Their stiffest challenge came in the conference semifinals, where the New York Knicks attempted to emulate the tactics once used by the Pistons with such success.

But Jordan had learned how to win. When his teammates, especially Pippen, showed signs of wilting

Following the 1992 season, Jordan suited up as a member of the USA basketball team at the Olympic Games in Barcelona, Spain, along with such fellow luminaries as Larry Bird, Magic Johnson, Charles Barkley, and Patrick Ewing. The so-called Dream Team easily won the gold medal; the toughest competition Jordan and his teammates faced came in intrasquad games in practices.

The King of Hoops goes one-on-one with the King of Pop: Jordan prepares to make a move on Michael Jackson in a video for the singer's record Jam, *which was released in June 1992. With basketball poised to overtake soccer as the world's most popular sport, Jordan's worldwide celebrity rivals Jackson's.*

in the face of New York's relentless physical attack by complaining about the refereeing and underhanded tactics and otherwise displaying signs of intimidation, Jordan offered advice and support rather than criticism. "If you go in the paint, you're going to get hit," he counseled. "But you have to go in the paint." When Knicks' tough guy Xavier McDaniel began bouncing Pippen around the court, it was Jordan, not one of the bigger Bulls, who got in McDaniel's face with an expletive-filled tirade to let him know the Bulls would not be pushed around. When Pippen was heavily criticized in the media for his soft play, Jordan offered public support. In the end, none of Jordan's teammates played very well against the Knicks, but they did not disappear, and they added enough to Jordan's superlative play to allow Chicago to prevail in an exceptionally hardfought seven games.

The championship series with the Portland Trailblazers was heralded as a one-on-one showdown between Jordan and Clyde Drexler, his counterpart at shooting guard. Although some in the media had had the temerity to suggest that Drexler was Jordan's

The best basketball player in the world: Jordan dances atop the scorer's table in Chicago on June 14, 1992, in celebration of the Bulls's second straight NBA championship.

equal or even his better as the NBA's best all-around player, the match-up proved ludicrously one-sided. In just the first half of the first game, Michael torched Clyde for an NBA-record 35 points, including an NBA-record six three-point field goals. Drexler never recovered; he spent the rest of the series trailing after Jordan and forcing bad shot after bad shot, and his team lost in six games. Jordan's thorough dominance of the league's second-best player was simply astonishing; never had the gap between himself and his peers been made so manifestly clear. Whereas once it had been charged that Jordan's on-court character would prevent him from attaining true greatness, now that same character was seen as being even more essential to his success than his superlative physical gifts. Jordan's greatness, wrote Philadelphia sportswriter Bill Lyon, "has not so much to do with talent, as it does with temperament. Jordan, by nature, will take a game and mold it in his hands, and he will lash his teammates, goad them, shame them."

In the postseason, Jordan gathered his trophies—his second straight as the league's MVP, his second straight as MVP of the playoffs, his sixth straight as scoring leader, his second straight championship ring, and even a second Olympic gold medal, as a member of the 1992 U.S. Olympic basketball team. As the jingle to his new Gatorade commercial advised kids to "be like Mike," there were new criticisms—revelations that he gambled, for exceptionally high stakes, on golf and cards; characterizations of him, most specifically in Sam Smith's *The Jordan Rules*, as relentlessly competitive and driven; charges that he blackballed Isiah Thomas from the Olympic squad; slams from teammates for failing to show at the White House after an invitation from President George Bush. His great wealth and fame had not been achieved without cost; his time was rarely his own, and by most accounts his celebrity forced him to live a life near isolation. But on the court, there were still moments of incomparable beauty and grace and wonder—the shrug of the shoulders and palms-up gesture made to Magic Johnson, who was working the game as an announcer, after the sixth and final three-pointer in the first half of the first game against Portland, as if, finally, Jordan had amazed even himself—and Jordan's rules had become the on-court standard by which all other players had to measure themselves.

Despite occasional talks of retirement, occasioned by the unrelenting scrutiny to which his on- and offcourt life was now subjected, Jordan entered the 1992–93 season more driven than ever. Though the Bulls managed only the league's third-best record in the regular season, they regrouped in the playoffs and sucessfully defended their crown. In the finals against Pheonix, Jordan averaged an incomparable 41 points over six games, including a magnificent 55 points in game four, and won his third straight playoff-MVP award; no other player has even won it so much as twice in succession.

Just several days before the Bulls began training camp in October 1993, Jordan stunned the world by announcing his retirement from basketball. Speculation as to his reason focused on the death of his beloved father, who had been brutally murdered that past summer. The reason was much simpler, Jordan said. There were no more challenges for him on the court.

Instead, he took up an old love and a new challenge: baseball. At the age of 31, Jordan became a minor league ballplayer in the Chicago White Sox organization. Although his first season was hardly a success, Jordan vowed to pursue his dream of becoming a major leaguer. After all, didn't he always accomplish what he set his mind on? ❧